UNBINDING
Love

A Guide for the Caregiver
Who Has Nothing Left to Give

Rebecca
STEWART

Copyright © 2021 by Rebecca Stewart

Unbinding Love

All rights reserved. No part of this publication may be reproduced, distributed, or transmitted in any form or by any means, including photocopying, recording, or other electronic or mechanical methods, without the prior written permission of the publisher, except in the case of brief quotations embodied in critical reviews and certain other noncommercial uses permitted by copyright law.

Although the author and publisher have made every effort to ensure that the information in this book was correct at press time, the author and publisher do not assume and hereby disclaim any liability to any party for any loss, damage, or disruption caused by errors or omissions, whether such errors or omissions result from negligence, accident, or any other cause.

Adherence to all applicable laws and regulations, including international, federal, state, and local governing professional licensing, business practices, advertising, and all other aspects of doing business in the US, Canada, or any other jurisdiction is the sole responsibility of the reader and consumer.

Neither the author nor the publisher assumes any responsibility or liability whatsoever on behalf of the consumer or reader of this material. Any perceived slight of any individual or organization is purely unintentional.

The resources in this book are provided for informational purposes only and should not be used to replace the specialized training and professional judgment of a healthcare or mental healthcare professional.

Neither the author nor the publisher can be held responsible for the use of the information provided within this book. Please always consult a trained professional before making any decision regarding treatment of yourself or others.

ISBN: 978-1-7365736-1-7

DEDICATION

This book is dedicated to my mom Lainey. You are a warrior and hummingbird all at once. You loved me when I needed you the most, and I will love you when you need me the most.

Tell me in the morning about your love,
Because I trust you.
Show me what I should do,
Because my prayers go up to you.

Psalm 143:8 NCV

TABLE OF CONTENTS

Preface 1

Introduction: The Chaos of Caregiving 7

Faith

Chapter 1: The Gift 21

Grace

Chapter 2: Allowing God to Build You Up 47

Surrender

Chapter 3: Let Go and Let God 67

Grace

Chapter 4: The Ones We Care for Have the Power to Bring Us Down 99

Hope

Chapter 5: What You Can Do to Make a Difference ... 121

Chapter 6: A Final Prayer for You 173

Acknowledgments 179

About the Author 181

PREFACE

This book almost didn't happen. I started writing it in August of 2019. I was hopeful and felt moved by the Holy Spirit when present at a Bible study at my church, the Lord asked me to share my story with others so that they may have hope about mental illness. I could have given up on this project a half a dozen times, being a home educator, taking care of kids, being a guardian to my mom, going through COVID-19 in the spring of 2020, and being a single mom for almost three months because my husband was protecting us from the possible exposure of coronavirus through his workplace of nearly 200 people. My children missed their daddy, I kept writing, teaching, cooking, cleaning, and praying God would deliver us from this horrible predicament.

I watched friends disagree on the validity of masks. I watched our nation get divided over race issues, politics, and Trump supporters vs non supporters, and I watched horrific natural disasters such as an inland hurricane completely demolish the state of Iowa. All of this turmoil turned me into a puddle of a mess. It was difficult to remain hopeful that God would provide. Fear and doubt gripped me like a hawk around its prey. I couldn't sleep at night. I couldn't make some deadlines with the book. I began to question if this book was really ever going to help anyone.

Hebrews 11:11 says, "Sarah's faith embraced the miracle power to conceive even though she was barren and was past the age of childbearing, for the authority of her faith rested in the One who made the promise, and she tapped into his faithfulness." If Sarah had the strength and courage to ask God for His divine help in becoming a mom, to do the impossible, then surely I had the right to ask God to make my path straight if I just got up early in the morning to finish this book. Being a night owl meant I had to set my alarm early for 5:30 a.m. and allow the Holy Spirit to help me write on these pages. Once I made it clear to the Lord that I would be getting up early, He would help me create this book. We made a pact.

Along with the fear of COVID-19 came the realization that my role as caregiver for my mother, Lainey, was also changing. I was no longer allowed into her nursing home and I had been used to daily visits. I loved walking in and making her smile. Holding her hand and reading scripture to her on Sunday mornings. We had such a connection, such a bond that I will never experience with another human being on this planet. It was complicated and it was hard, as many mother-daughter relationships can be. It was hard watching my mom mentally and physically deteriorate in a nursing home. But I didn't realize how special it was to just be able to visit because I took it for granted! Of course I could come inside, I was her guardian and had every right to check up on her to make sure her clothing was clean and her needs were taken care of. That she knew I was there, that was just a given. But my last visit to my mom took place on Feb 25, 2020. It was like any other visit. I came and she was asleep in her room. I put my hand on her head and said a silent prayer. I let her sleep because why wake her? There would be plenty more visits... or so I thought. Then on March 11, 2020, the World

PREFACE

Health Organization announced COVID-19 as a pandemic after the disease spread to more than 100 countries and led to tens of thousands of cases in a few months. The nursing home had to protect the vulnerable occupants inside, but it was gut wrenching to think about my mom inside a building where I had no access to for the first time ever.

I remained hopeful and carried on with the work of the book because in a spiritual way it kept me connected to my mother. She knew I was writing this book, in fact when I told her I was sharing our story she smiled and said, "You're special!" It warmed my heart and I carried that with me on cold nights when I wondered about my mom's condition.

The nursing home allowed FaceTime video chats, but a lot of the time she was distracted. It did not compare at all to physically touching her hand, but it allowed me to see she was safe and that meant a lot. Finally, on August 25th 2020 at 10 a.m., I was granted an outdoor visit with my mom. It had been six months since I had seen her last. I actually felt extremely nervous beforehand. I wore a pretty dress and took off my sunglasses so she could see my eyes. When she came out of the building being pushed by a wheelchair, my heart sunk. She was not in a wheelchair before COVID. It was so wonderful and heartbreaking at the same time because all that connection had been lost. She knew who I was, but she was frail and she had a hard time keeping eye contact with me. Also, I was wearing a mask so it was hard for her to see my whole face. She was sweet but distant, and after about ten minutes she asked to go back inside. My heart broke. I kindly said it would be okay, smiled, and told her I loved her. Walking back to my car I burst into tears. It was a hard blow, and I realized I was experiencing a new level of grief with her. It triggered other moments when I felt grief over my mom's illness, over a change in her, over losing a part of her again. I was too grief stricken to drive so I sat in my car and let all the tears come out. I got on my phone and messaged my closest friends and family and asked them for prayer.

God has a way of healing and mending our hearts. I realize now that this is the new start of our relationship. COVID-19 may have changed our connection, but it did not change the love I have for my mother.

This morning, Tuesday September 2nd, I will be bringing one of her granddaughters with me to have another outdoor visit with Lainey. I am hopeful that we can start building up a relationship again in a new capacity that I never envisioned would take place. And the snow is coming ... so we have to get these visits going!

What was your COVID story like? Did you lose connection with your loved one? Did you feel lost and alone? Please share your stories with me and send me an email to info@unbindinglove.com. I want to hear how you are doing now.

Your author and friend,
Rebecca Stewart

Introduction

THE CHAOS OF CAREGIVING

---

*"Can all your worries add a
single moment to your life?"*

–Matthew 6:27 NLT

You were meant to live a life of ease, peace, and tranquility. My guess is right now you are not feeling those feelings. Many of us as caregivers are burdened with the responsibility of looking after a loved one, and that burden is so great that we lose ourselves in the process. If you are feeling overwhelmed (to the point that you've forgotten who you are, who God intended you to be, what YOUR dreams are and your goals in the future), you have been robbed of the goodness that God intended you to have. You, my friend, are in what's called "burn out." Many caregivers, even those who do not live with their loved one, experience these sleepless nights of feeling tremendous guilt, worry, and anxiety over situations that they have zero control over.

You see, I became my mom's legal guardian in May 2004 while studying in college at the University of Wisconsin-Madison. When asked to come to my mom's court hearing, I went not realizing the judge would deem my mother mentally incompetent and request someone present at the meeting to become her guardian. Since I was the only family member present, the judge deemed me guardian of person and estate for my mother. I was in shock! I was a typical college student: I had a boyfriend and worked two jobs. I was tempted to skip class to stay home and watch my favorite TV shows. I wanted to be a little bit more independent, but I was still developing and figuring life out for myself. I was a normal college student except now I had a major responsibly, my mother.

I basically became a parent to my own parent. I was now in charge of her entire well-being, which included having regular meetings with her social worker, doctor, care team, and SSI. I didn't even know what SSI was. (It's financial government assistance) If there was a medication change, I needed to approve it. I had to balance her checkbook, pay her bills, report to the county every year where her money went via the annual report (her version of taxes). I drove 120 miles to my hometown on the weekends to help clean out my mom's refrigerator from rotten broccoli and clean her smelly clothes (What happens to you when you're on psych meds). She had gotten to the point where she couldn't take care of herself anymore. She started streaking down the hallways naked. She was constantly confused, eating the same foods for each meal, leaving the oven on, and forgetting what month it was. Early onset dementia is what the doctor called it. She was given a brain scan and diagnosed with Alzheimer's. She was only 60 years old.

Looking back, I was completely unaware of the responsibility I was signing up for. No one told me that by October, two months before my graduation, I would have to move my mom into assisted living, a CBRF (community-based residential facility), somehow move all her items that she had collected for over 50 years, downsize to a one-bedroom home, and still have her talking to me by the end of the process. She was not ready for the move, and I had no idea how to move her. It was a recipe for disaster.

I spent weeks trying to develop a plan to move my mom safely and without too much upset. I told myself that it was no big deal and that anyone could do this. But I was a nervous wreck! I spent nights lying awake, grabbing more Post-it Notes and jotting down reminders I would have to remember the next day. Things like "Don't forget Mom's favorite Blessed Mary statue. Don't forget her favorite slippers. Remember to have her rosary next to her bed." Oh yeah, and the precious Kincaid bedroom set she had saved up for and owned for years would not fit inside her humble one-bedroom home. I had to donate it to the church because there was no room for it.

I had no money, so I went to Big Lots and purchased her a smaller and affordable bedroom set that would match the soft blue coloring of the walls. I planned out every decor element, without ever having done it before for myself, as I had only lived with other messy roommates in dingy dorm rooms and tiny apartments adorned with college appropriate furnishings. In other words, I had no idea what I was doing. In desperation, I sent my mom to her mom's house who was 91 years old at the time. I asked my grandma if she could watch my mom for a week so I could get Mom's belongings moved out of her very large and filled to the brim one-bedroom apartment and move her into this teeny tiny one bedroom in the new CBRF (community-based residential facility). Thankfully, my grandma agreed.

Now I had seven days to move my mom. I called friends in a panic looking for some moral support. All in their early 20's like me, no one had any advice on how to move their parent into assisted living. It would be the first major decision I'd have to make for my mother on her behalf and I felt completely clueless as to how to do it. Not only was I winging it, I had to somehow do it all behind her back because she was not mentally able to process or make decisions on her own. I certainly could have talked to her ahead of time, but due to my youth, inexperience, and fear of opposition from her, I went ahead and made rash decisions by the seat of my pants. With eyes closed like riding a rollercoaster into unknown territory, I knew I was headed for trouble. I felt nervous, alone, scared, and totally out of my comfort zone. I knew I had the potential here to really mess things up with my mom. Would she trust me after doing this? Would she forgive me? I hoped and prayed somehow by the grace of God everything would be just fine.

As you can imagine, with knots in my stomach, things weren't magically fine. I remember the week before I moved my mom, I popped such a huge cold sore on my lip from all the stress. I just had to get this over with. I was trying to wrap up my college degree and get ready for graduation in December. The pressure was on at school, and the pressure was on to get my mom moved safely into her new home. Like jumping out of an airplane at 13,000 feet, I took a deep breath and took the plunge. Within a few days, I gave away about 80% of her things, donated most of her furniture, set up her new room, and I did this without asking for help from anyone else. I don't know why I felt I had to do it all on my own.

Now it was time to tell my mom and take her to her new home. I picked my mom up from my grandma's house on a Sunday morning and drove her back to our hometown. It was an agonizing two-hour drive as my mom, oblivious to what was about to happen, continued on her conversation regarding the visit with her mom. How was I going to break the news and tell her that she had no apartment anymore?

We drove to Menomonee Park, a familiar place we went to on warm summer days, and as we pulled over and turned off the car, I told my mom we needed to have a talk. I explained to her that she had a new home now. I don't remember her response other than it was complete shock for her. "I don't have an apartment anymore?" Was all she could get out. My heart sunk for her.

Although my mom loved her new room and was ready to let go of the burden of cooking and cleaning for herself, she was not mentally prepared for the major change that just crashed into her life. Even though I was not equipped (not by any means), I somehow successfully moved her into assisted living. I slept in her bed with her for the first night and spent many days checking over her to make sure she was comfortable. It took months and years for her to get adjusted to her new life. But she had no other choice.

Instead of focusing on my finals and upcoming college graduation, I had been tediously planning out my mother's life and her next chapter of living less independently. Assessing her needs, assessing her wants, I was hardly thinking about my professors or college friends or the Wisconsin Badger football team. I was playing social worker, parent, daughter, and friend all in one. And it was exhausting. I wasn't partying or finding myself or going on backpack adventure trips through Europe like my friends were. I was getting daily migraines, experiencing sleepless nights, and lying awake wondering when the next time my mom would call or need something or worse ... need hospitalization. It was a cycle I had no control over. I had no idea how to be a caregiver for my mom or how to set boundaries with her so that I could achieve the true balance I needed to be a successful legal guardian. No, I was winging it, and I continued to wing it for over a decade before I found a system and a rhythm that worked.

There were no books to teach me how to be a parent to my parent. Forget the emotional hurt over that concept and the sheer awkwardness of parenting your parent while you still need parenting yourself. At the time, I was still growing and developing and needed a mother to help me sort out my life, what I wanted to be when I grew up. I wanted a mom to take me shopping. I wanted to be cherished and praised over the small areas of success in my life like graduating from a four-year university. My mother wasn't able to give that to me. Worse, I wasn't tapping into God's word or his promises, and I wasn't surrendering. Not at all! I was moving full speed ahead into the wall called "burn out." We all know what that wall feels like to collide with. Not fun.

I'm writing this book to share the wisdom with you that I've learned over the struggling years. You, the caregiver, the family member, who are facing daily challenges and are ready to throw in the towel. The problem with my early years of caregiving is I didn't understand the rhythm and balance of establishing good and healthy boundaries with my mom so that I could handle all of the hurdles coming our way. In the 20 years that I've been taking care of my mom, I've learned so many helpful tips that I think are simple and easy to do, yet life changing. Would you like to know more?

Today I am my mom's guardian and caregiver, but I have peace and joy in my life about it. I cherish her and the role I have in supporting her without losing myself. I have established the groundwork so I can focus on important priorities in my life like my family, friends, and my faith. I still am an emotional provider for her, but I enjoy it! I am drinking a full cup and living life out of abundance and not scarcity. It is caretaking at its best.

Who This Book Is For

This book is for anyone who is struggling with the burden of loving someone with a debilitating illness. My journey is caring for someone with a severe mental illness, but for you it may be different. This book will especially benefit the Schizophrenia Caregiver: For the mother who's got an adult son living out of his car, who has stopped communicating to her for months. For the father who now has to raise his daughter alone because his spouse was recently diagnosed and isn't on medication and has disappeared from their lives. For the girlfriend who fell in love with her boyfriend who has the illness, and he leaves her confused and hopeless because he falls in and out of love with her based on the direction of the wind or whatever mood or voice he is listening to that day.

This book is for the weary. The one who comes with a tired heart. The one who's looking for some answers. Any answers, because their loved one tried new medication that won't help, or they had to stop paying rent for their daughter because they can't afford it and worry if she will go homeless tomorrow. For the lost. For the angry one. For the caregiver who says they are on the brink of madness themselves because they've lost who they are, what their purpose is, and what the heck God made them for to be put on this earth.

Maybe you don't have a life. Maybe you've given everything over to your loved one. Maybe you are afraid if you make changes you will have to say no or you will have to be wrong or make a mistake. Maybe you are tired of having to think. Then this book is for you. If you think you have it all together, or you think miraculously life will get better, that your loved one will stay on their medications for the rest of their lives and never have psychosis again, then this book isn't for you. This book is for the sick and tired, down and out, lost and forgotten caregiver. You are not alone. You are not forgotten. This book may be radical to some and simple to others. I believe the simplicity in this book outlined for the caregiver is made to be simple so it can be applied and life changing. All it takes is some time and some faith. If you have time to read the words on this page, then you have time to start putting yourself back on the to-do list.

God the Father sees you in your state, and His awareness causes Him deep grief. He sees you and your hurt heart. He knows your suffering. It's time you understood His deep love and the power of His voice when you seek to hear it. This book is a guide to hearing that voice. To stick up for yourself. To unbinding the love you have for yourself by seeking out a higher power. The love is for you. You may have seen the title of this book and assumed it was meant for the one you look after. No, it is the undying love you have from the Father. How can the pain of loving someone with a debilitating illness bring you to the Father? *Because you have nowhere else to turn to.* Because it's been there all along. Maybe you have already been tapping into the Holy Spirit. Maybe you have already been praying every day. Or maybe this is the first time you've even heard of such a thing as the Holy Spirit. Either way, this is a personal invitation for you to come to the profound healing and unbinding love from the Father.

Why Believe Me?

Lord knows I've made a lot of mistakes being the caregiver and guardian to my mother. I've been taking care of her for over 30 years and have been guardian for 18. It has been heavy and exhausting. It has caused me so much anxiety. In my youth, I did the best I could, but I was a mess. I had no clue what I was doing. I felt sorry for myself all the time. I was like the princess in the highest tower of the castle. No one had access to me because I was too busy crying in my corner of Schizophrenia. **I believed the lie that my life would never be normal because it was tainted by the stain of mental illness. I had no idea that God was using this devastating journey to sharpen my mind, my heart, and my eyes to the vision and life path He set out for me to have.** The path that led me to a movement. The movement is discovering my own self, that I'm a strong woman capable of great things. That I am *not* defined by mental illness, my mother, or any other earthly thing. My definition in the dictionary is only written by my creator. No one else has the right.

The movement is this book and the opportunity I have through Christ to bring this message of hope to you. You are so very special and were created to do great things.

God set out for you to be a caregiver to someone very special to Him. He knew you could do it, in time, with patience and practice and wisdom. This mission is temporary; for as long as you live on this earthly planet or your loved one lives, you are given a short mission of providing love and care to someone else more vulnerable than you. You can take His calling and do the best. You can be easy on yourself and give yourself the grace and the breathing room to make mistakes. You can let go of perfection, other people's opinions, societal views, everything. How freeing life can get when you let go of all that mental garbage that weighs on your mind and yet holds no spiritual value.

Right now, you need to let that all go. Let go of assumptions, grudges, fear, and anger. There is no room left in your heart for that. Instead, open your heart to one source. And that source is Christ the King. He is the Mighty Lion, and He doesn't love you just a little. His love is fierce and personal and profound! He wastes no time handing over His love to you. He is like a mother bear to her cub. With one big swipe, He moves obstacles and mountains out of our way. Wouldn't you like to make more room for that kind of love in your life? I'm going to show you how.

"You are my King, O God; Command victories for Jacob. Through You we will push down our enemies; Through Your name we will trample those who rise up against us. For I will not trust in my bow, Nor shall my sword save me. But you have saved us from our enemies. And have put to shame those who hated us. In God we boast all day long And praise Your name forever." –Psalm 44:4–8

Throughout the book, we will be focusing on the four pillars of caregiving: faith, grace, surrender, and hope. These four pillars are the foundation for purposeful and well-balanced caregiving. Without receiving these blessings, we will not be able to create care from a rested state. I'm going to show you specific examples of achieving these qualities in your life so you can be the caregiver God created you to be.

Faith

The Gift

Chapter 1
THE GIFT

"You are a chosen people, a royal priesthood, a holy nation, God's special possession."
–1 Peter 2:9 NIV

The morning sun began to peek over the distant hills behind our tiny house. Our house was situated on Campbell Creek, a marshy area of nothing next to a large college football stadium. In the summertime at night, you could hear the announcer, music, and excitement from the game. However, now all you could hear was the stillness of winter as the sun slowly moved its way from hiding below the earth. The rabbits were hiding among the bushes warm in their burrows. The geese had long been gone, and all that remained of summer was the occasional black bird that searched the ground for anything close to resembling a worm. The sky was a dark navy blue with hints of desert pink just waiting to bloom into the bright marigolds of the sky. The world was not awake yet but I was. Only five years old, I had a habit of waking up before my mother. I gazed across the bedroom to observe if she lay undisturbed. Of course she was, because every morning included her sleeping in until noon.

My eyes were still crusty from slumber, like the stubbornness of a flower waiting to bloom. I looked up at the old white ceiling with paint chipping off. It had grown weary too from the harsh Wisconsin subzero temperatures. The bedroom was decorated with 1970s farmhouse-like decor that helped the room look charming despite the ugly faux wood paneling that covered the walls. The bedroom furniture was dark wood and kept shiny. My mother kept a tidy home. I had a small wooden twin size bed my father made for me out of pine, lodged against one wall so as to not take up too much space. It wasn't a box spring or double mattress, just hard wood with a tiny mattress on top. Yet as uncomfortable as it must have been, my mother's comfort made up for it.

Each night she slept next to me in her queen-sized bed, a four-corner poster princess bed that matched the Kincaid hutch alongside the wall. Behind her bed were two large windows that led out to the front porch. In the summertime, it was beastly hot because my mother didn't believe in air conditioning. In the winter, the cold air easily leaked through the poorly insulated window panes. On top of the hutch lay an old depression glass lamp, cream with the picture of a beautiful rose in the center. Feminine and neat just like my mother. And a tiny black radio that only had AM/FM and a cassette player. She had inside it an Elvis Presley Christmas tape. Also on the hutch was a picture of the Blessed Mary in the corner of my mother's mirror.

As I crept with warm feet on the icy wooden floor, I tiptoed quietly like a mouse from one end of the bedroom to the next, and as I approached two steps from exiting the bedroom, I started to run with excitement because I had just escaped the boring room. As I headed around the corner to the living room, I gazed up at the modest sized artificial Christmas tree my mom had placed next to our couch on the far side of the wall. It was strung with twinkly Christmas lights and had a baby Jesus below the branches nestled in a basket on the floor. On top of the tree, something new that hadn't been there before glistened in the morning light. As I rubbed my eyes to get a better look at it, I was overcome with joy. Racing as fast as my little legs could run, I laid my eyes on the most beautiful object I had ever seen. Sitting on top of the tree was a silver tiara, handmade with tiny diamond-like sequins sewn all around it. And it was mine sent directly from God.

You see, the night before during my bedtime prayers, I asked God to *please* give me a beautiful princess tiara for Christmas. As a child, toys were scarce. My mother and I lived off public assistance. We drank powdered milk and ate pea soup for eight days in a row. I was not a spoiled child by any means. I did not own any dolls, or barbies, or pound puppies. But all I really wanted was a tiara so I could pretend I was a princess and dream I lived in a castle and could afford any toy I wanted. Imagination is everything to a child. So is possibility—the possibility to be anything you want to be, regardless of circumstance. Regardless of chance. I wanted a tiara, and my mother had just made a magnificent miracle happen. Or Jesus ... whomever you want to give the credit to.

From that day on, my faith in the Lord was strong. I knew He really listened to me and gave me that beautiful present. My mother always read to me the Bible and taught me about our Loving God and how He loves us so much He would do anything for us. In that moment, I had a tangible reason to love the Lord. I still love the Lord today, but my understanding runs deeper now. I give that credit to my steadfast and selfless mother who quickly made the decision to make my day. She didn't have the money to give me a Christmas present early. She was not frivolous, but she knew a good opportunity when she saw one. My heart fills with joy when I think about her love for me then. Later on in the year, she had professional pictures taken of me wearing the tiara she made with her own two hands. It is the most precious picture of me as a child. Beaming from ear to ear, I was someone who was loved by God. I never doubted the Lord's devotion to me after that. Little did we know, my mother and I would be severed soon after and I would desperately need that faith. We would never be mother daughter in the same capacity again. Never would I be small and she be big.

THE GIFT

Several months went by and summer was barely hanging on by a thread. Our tiny house on Jackson Avenue began to resemble a zoo. Dishes lay scattered on the counters, the cat was meowing from missing her meals, and piles of clothing covered the bedroom and bathroom floor. My mother stopped sleeping at night. Whenever I woke up, she was either not in the room or laying wide eyed. Once I caught her standing next to the bed banging on her hip with a hammer. She said it helped her relieve some pain from when her and my dad were in a car accident years ago.

I was now in the first grade at Franklin Elementary School and Mrs. Watson became concerned when I came to class without my spelling workbook. I told her I wouldn't be coming to school with books anymore because my mother had thrown all of them away. I said I did something really bad and my mommy became upset with me so she tossed them. The teacher never spoke another word to me. Even though she gave me all new textbooks, my world did not get any better.

That afternoon when the bus dropped me off, I found my mother sitting on the edge of her bed, staring down at the tiny black radio on her hutch. "It's magic," she said in a far-off land voice. At first, I thought she was acting out like the fairy Godmother in Cinderella. I was waiting for her to look up at me and snap out of it. But she didn't. She told me to sit down and wait for it. "Wait for it?" I repeated feeling a little puzzled. "Becky, this is important! Sit down right now next to me. Oh my God! It's magic. Magic 104." The local radio station 104 that played all the modern pop was playing on my mother's radio and she thought it was the most amazing miracle. After repeating it four more times, I became bored. "Mom, nothing is happening." I said with an annoyed tone. My mother sat for hours like this. It was at this point I became really desperate.

First off, it was supper time and I was hungry. I opened the refrigerator and immediately became overwhelmed by the smell of rotten food. I tried making a bowl of cereal but the milk had gone bad. After nibbling on bits of cheese and some old potato chips, I felt content. I decided I would do something nice for my mom in an attempt to make her feel better. I grabbed the small coffee percolator and made my mom a stiff cup of coffee. It still had coffee grains floating on top, but I was pretty proud of it. Holding the mug, I carefully brought it into the bedroom, determined not to make a spill. My mother was no longer in the same world as me. She didn't even notice my gesture or seem to hear what I had to say.

"Mom, look! I brought you a nice warm cup of coffee. Why don't you come out in the kitchen and have a bite to eat and relax?" Her eyes became large like saucers. At this point, she became completely mute and refused to talk to me. Apparently, she was not in the mood to eat or drink either. I shrugged and brought the cup of coffee back to the kitchen. Hurt and disappointed my plan didn't work, I dumped the coffee down the sink and looked out the kitchen window at the beautiful pond of Campbell Creek. I grabbed my light jean coat and went outside to watch the sunset. I could hear the comforting and familiar sounds of the crickets and the frogs croaking along the tall grass. Maybe things weren't the same inside the house, but they sure were outside of it. I walked out on the dock where my grandpa showed me how to cast a fishing pole. I wished my gramps was with me right now. I wished someone could help my mom feel better. As night time approached, a gusty wind blew musty dust in my face and eyes.

Exhausted and overwhelmed by the day, I pulled back my long blond hair and stood tall with strength. "I am alright," I kept telling myself. "I know how to put myself to bed."

I don't think I got a lot of sleep that night, but I'm not sure because everything goes blank. The brain has ways of erasing bad memories, it's called self-protection. I don't know exactly what happened that night. What I do know for sure is before the week was done, my dad would rescue me like a prince in an old beaten up pickup truck, and I would never return to our house or live with my mother again.

This is the age of my life that caretaking began for me. Even though I was a small child, I knew my mother needed care. I also put her needs in front of my own. I worried about her when she didn't sleep. I remember making her coffee a lot, trying to comfort her, when I was the one that needed comforting.

The reason why I start my caretaking story from here is because this is when it began for me. I was not fully capable of taking care of my mother and all her needs because I was only a child. However, now I am a full-grown adult, and I know that God has equipped me with all the tools I need to be there for her today.

First Off, Are YOU Capable?

God wants you to know you are mighty and capable of the loving caregiving you need to provide. You are enough. There is no such thing as perfect caregiving. Only God is capable of miracle working and the perfection that you are seeking. God has given you a special mission, a special act on earth that only a few have the privilege to do. It's so special and rare to be called on this journey. It is hard and it is a burden, but it is beautiful. God knows you have a special heart. He has faith that you can do it. God is sad that Satan has gotten ahold of caregivers. He's breathing lies into them and robbing them of joy by implanting the thought that they are not good enough.

Mental Illness Is a Spiritual Struggle

No matter which end you look at it, whether from the perspective of the mentally ill patient or the caregiver, mental illness will challenge everything you think about life and all hope in the future. This spiritual struggle is the hardest struggle I have ever had to personally witness, and it holds such power to kill, steal, and destroy the joy in our lives. Anything that holds that much power over us can only be behind one thing. Now I am not saying mental illnesses like Schizophrenia are a demon. I am saying it has the power to steal the goodness from our lives, and that is a big problem. It is a problem that seeks to take all faith and hope we have in our hearts and crush it like a peanut underneath a monster truck. It smashes all hope and leaves us with the pieces. And if we're not careful, it will feed us the lie that we are powerless against Schizophrenia and unable to change a thing. "He will never stay on his meds. What's the point? She can't even carry out a conversation with me so why try? Why ask questions when he only provides the same answer over and over with a blank stare." These are lies that Satan tells us to squelch our spirit and make it easy to give up.

What if I told you there was a way you can still communicate with your loved one, even if they are unable to talk back? Even if they are sick, in psychosis, angry, or suicidal, you can still connect with them. Would you do it? Would you seek connection with your loved one? Would you be open to a new perspective, a new reality that allowed you some peace? This book will show you step by step how to have peace and acceptance within yourself. It will also help give you the tools you can implement to start healing on your journey as a caregiver to someone with Schizophrenia.

How Does a Loving God Allow Mental Illness?

How could God be okay with mental illness on His beautiful planet? He created the Earth and saw that it was good. Why create a human being and allow this condition, this darkness, this evil to take away the good of a person to only replace it with hardship? Well, you can go one step further. Why does God allow murder, rape, genocide, and even natural disasters like earthquakes to happen to crush us like ants? How could a God who loves us so much allow this to happen? The answer is simple and biblical.

God allows us to suffer because it's the human condition since Adam and Eve. Humans had free will, free choice to do whatever they wanted. They had the garden and the animals, and everything in the beginning was a utopia of existence. Then Satan came. In Genesis, the Bible says Satan came in the form of a serpent, a snake, and he tricked Adam and Eve into believing it was okay to eat the fruit because then they would be more like God. Satan, in today's world, still has that ability to get you where you're weak. He'll accuse you of believing lies about yourself, and he'll cause you to doubt good. He'll try to make you turn away from the thought that God is good. He'll be the one telling you that because your loved one has this terrible mental illness, surely there isn't a good and loving God. If you've ever believed that, and I know I have, then the enemy was hard at work. But deep down, we know that can't be true, because we know in the Bible it says God loves us so much that he sacrificed his child Jesus for us!

"We love because He first loved us." –1 John 4:19

In my own life, as a young child, I remember witnessing my mom struggle with her faith. She'd go to church and pray for God to heal her, help her, and hear her, only to return home to her apartment and cry on her couch for hours. I remember as a young child, about age seven, feeling so helpless and sorry for her. She clearly had struggles and problems that she felt weren't being addressed. The feeling of helplessness that came over me was so crippling, and I knew only God had the power to really help my mom. But would He do it? In the Bible it says that God does not heal everyone. He deep down loves us and wants the best for us, but the ultimate choice is still up to Him.

In order to understand why there is sickness in the world, you need to first understand the history of the world. When God created the world, he had *no* intentions of evil, sickness, or disease. He created man and woman (Adam and Eve) to live in the garden and thrive and be happy. He also had a relationship with them. Can you imagine that? It is very difficult to do because all we know in this life is a fallen world. However, in the Bible, it clearly says in the beginning all was good. There was no sin, and Adam and Eve roamed around the garden naked and free and were not ashamed of their naked bodies, their flaws, or their situation. Then the enemy came in. He tricked them into believing that maybe what God told them wasn't the truth. Here enters doubt. Tell me, how many times in your life have you been crippled with doubt? Too many times to say.

Everyone today experiences doubt. For Adam and Eve, this was the first time they experienced doubt about what God was telling them regarding the fruit. The serpent tricked Eve into believing that if she ate the fruit of knowledge she'd be more like God. So she did it. Not only did she do it, she talked Adam into doing it! From that moment on, their eyes knew they were naked, and in their hearts, they trembled with fear from the Lord. Like a toddler who stole a cookie from the cookie jar, Eve knew what she did was wrong. So what did God do? Did He turn his back on creation? Did He abandon human life? NO. He cried and felt the pain of evil, too, but instead of turning away from Adam and Eve, He pursued further a relationship with them. He did not turn away. He still loved them because they were His children. From that point on, sin and darkness and evil fell upon the earth. That is why we have sickness, depression, and natural disasters. God doesn't want these things to happen to us; He doesn't create darkness for us. He weeps with us when we weep. He feels our pain, and He truly wants us to turn to him when we are in sorrow.

Some people believe that God uses suffering for us to turn to Him. I full heartedly believe that now, but there were many, many years that I couldn't because I didn't believe in the above explanation about creation. The story of Adam and Eve to me wasn't believable (Again, that's what Satan wants!). If you believe what the Bible says about creation and evil, then you can truly know and believe that Satan is behind all darkness on earth.

Many of us have an easier time believing in evil more so than having faith in God. Why is that? Just look around!

There is evil everywhere right? When you see little children sinning because they want what they want, then you know evil exists. They are still beautiful children, God's creation, but they are also flawed. No one has ever been perfect on Earth except for Jesus. Not Mother Teresa, not MLK Jr, not Ghandi. All sinners. It's weird to think of Mother Teresa as a sinner, but she was! When you see all the harsh stories broadcasted on the news, there is no denying evil in this world.

Did you know we are living in the most peaceful time in the world right now? Yes, that's right. There is proof that presently our world is at its most peaceful state compared to ancient times. Think of the Roman empire or the crusades, think of WW1 and WW2. Today we have the technology to broadcast all the bad news because let's face it, the bad news sells. No one wants to hear about the Boy Scout who helped the grandma with her groceries last Tuesday. But as soon as they write about a mother drowning her own infant, that's the click bait. Disgusting. We can login to Twitter and read about the negativity in the world, all the oppression, and all the unjust things. We feel a sick feeling in our stomachs, that feeling of dread and of helplessness. This is the enemy at work. You might ask, "Is the Enemy behind social media?" Yes! The enemy is behind everything. He is smart and deceptive, and he has his ways of sneaking into corners and alleyways. Social media is a breeze for him! So much openness and unprotected territory. Like a lamb freely roaming the pasture, a wolf comes only in a second to gobble it up. That's how Satan works.

The Lies Satan Tells Caregivers

You might as well just throw in the towel now; you can't handle your life and taking care of someone else's life.

You're going to go broke.

Family won't approve of your choices.

Your loved one will hate you.

There's no end to being a caregiver; you will be doing this forever.

You're missing out on the fun! You're missing out on enjoying your own life.

You can't make good decisions.

You're always late and you procrastinate.

There's no hope.

There are no good resources in your area.

You have no one you can trust.

You'll go crazy too!

And many, many more lies that Satan feeds us to deter us from our mission of helping out. What are the lies you have been told about yourself that you believe? If you have heard these lies, told yourself these lies, or believed these lies, then you need three helpful things—the Bible, faith, and this book. That's it. It's simple and it's effective, and I will show you all you need to do to change your mindset so you can be open to the **blessings of being a balanced caregiver.**

"Thus says the Lord who made it, the Lord who formed it to establish it, the Lord is His name: 'Call to Me, and I will answer you, and show you great and mighty things, which you do not know.'" –Jeremiah 33:2–3 NKJV

Prayer of Petition

Before we get into the nuts and bolts of this book, we need to first start with a prayer. Right now, you might be feeling alone and like life's knocked you down. You're tired and weary. Your Heavenly Father is waiting for you to come to Him, with the words He gave you in the Bible, through His son Jesus. He is the Way, the Truth, and the Life. He is the access to your living waters, and He will quench every thirst you have. Before we go a step further, I want to give you the opportunity to come to the Father. I want to introduce you to the powerful act of a prayer of petition. A prayer of petition is when you declare through God's word the truth that you shall not be overwhelmed anymore. You make a declaration through God's promises of what's going to take place from here on forward. Things are changing now. In order for things to change, you need to start with your brain and the acceptance that things will change. The old is gone and the new is here.

You might have already been praying for your loved one and for the situation to get better. While that's good, there is a more active and productive way to declare over your situation healing through Christ. You can pray this active prayer over any problem or situation over your life. For example, I have used it for help with my caregiving, and I have used it for help with my marriage. Satan loves to attack holy Christian marriages! I have used it to fight against my own fear of abandonment and feeling like I have to do everything on my own.

As a caregiver, we often feel like we're going through life alone. Like we're the only one having to give up ourselves for someone else. The truth is God knows what you are going through because He is always with you. But God also gives us free will to pray and to think and to act the way we believe we should. What a beautiful and creative father we have that He allows us this freedom! Sometimes it is almost too much freedom, because we don't know how to ask for what we need. I know in my life I have had a hard time asking God, friends, and family for help. But I know that I need the help. I know that I can't do it alone.

Why the Prayer of Petition Is the First Step

In order to set into motion the changes you will implement from this book, you first must believe a change has occurred through prayer. God says once you ask something of Him, it is already answered. Many of us pray in general to God, but we don't know how to come to Him and ask specifically for what we want. The clearer we are with the Lord, the better. When we come to Him with His word, His very own Bible verses, we are showing Him that not only do we understand His book of love but we are applying it to our lives. We are ready to learn from Him through His word and through His Holy Spirit. The Holy Spirit is a gift He gives us to help us on our path. This is an exciting first step and cannot be skipped.

You will need to get a notebook or a journal. At the top of the journal write "My Prayer of Petition." The Prayer of Petition has three parts:

1. Go to the written Word of God.
2. Consult with the Holy Spirit.
3. Write your petition.

Go to the Written Word

First, you must identify the number one issue you're facing right now. If it's fear, look up fear related Bible verses. If it's failure, lookup failure. I will give you a list of passages you may use for reference. Most bibles have a source in the back of the book that you can look up by subject. If not, just Google search. I will show you an example that you can use in your notebook to get started. Let's pretend you are struggling with a troubled heart. In general, you are feeling overwhelmed by your caregiving. At the top of the page, you will write:

Lord, You said in 2 Corinthians 1–3 that You are my merciful Father and the source of all comfort. You said You comfort us in all our troubles so that we can comfort others. When they are troubled, we will be able to give them the same comfort God has given us, for the more we suffer for Christ, the more God will shower us with his comfort through Christ. Lord, I'm asking for comfort today. I am troubled, Lord, and I need you right now.

Popular Bible Passages

Discernment—Hebrews 4:12, Philippians 1:9-10, Romans 12:2, 1 Corinthians 11:13–15

Dread—2 Timothy 3:17, Psalm 62:5-6, John 14:1–6, I Timothy 2:5, Jude 1:2

Fear—Isaiah 41:10, 2 Timothy 1:7, Psalm 34:4, Joshua 1:9

Failure—2 Corinthians 12:9–10, Romans 5:3–5, Psalm 73:26, Philippians 4:13

Self-Contempt—I John:1-9, Ephesians 5:29, Romans 5:1

Sadness—Psalm 35:9, Psalm 55:22, Jeremiah 29:11, Psalm 18:2, John 14:18

Lack of Awareness—2 Timothy 1:7, I Corinthians 6:19, Psalm 139:14, Philippians 4:13

Jealousy—Romans 12:2, Proverbs 14:30, I Peter 2:11

Indecisiveness—James 1:6, 2 Timothy 4:1–22, John 14:17

Hopelessness—Psalm 34:17–20, Jeremiah 29:11, Philippians 4:6–7, Luke 1:37

Meeting Another's Need Unselfishly—John 15:12, Philippians 2:4, James 1:27, Galatians 6:2

Supporting Others—Romans 5:1–21, Deuteronomy 22:4

Patience Without Anger—Galatians 6:9, Romans 8:25, Psalm 37:7–9

Caregiving—Philippians 4:13, 1 Corinthians 10:13, Romans 13:9, Acts 20:35

Mental Illness—Psalm 34:17–20, Philippians 4:6–7, 2 Timothy 1:7, Isaiah 41:10, John 16:33, 1 Peter 5:7, Jonah 2:5–7

Doing a Job When It Gets Tougher Than Expected—1 Corinthians 16:13

Applying Special Solutions to Special Problems—Luke 1:37, Romans 12:16, Matthew 11:28, Proverbs 3:5, Philippians 4:13

Moving Forward—1 Timothy 5:8, 1 Thessalonians 4:11–12, Ecclesiastes 9:10, Proverbs 25:26

Responsibility—Deuteronomy 28:1–68, Romans 12:3, 1 Corinthians 5:10, Galatians 6:2

Self Confidence—John 4:18, Philippians 4:13, 2 Timothy 1:7, Hebrews 13:6, Joshua 1:9, Psalm 139:13–14, Psalm 27:3, Proverbs 3:6, Philippians 4:4–7

Consult the Holy Spirit

The second step of the Prayer of Petition is to consult the Holy Spirit. Now this may seem foreign to you if you are a new believer. Maybe you didn't realize that once you receive Christ into your heart, you as a Christian believer are given access to Him always through the Holy Spirit. Whenever you need Him, He is waiting for you! Receive the Baptism in the Holy Spirit just as you received Jesus—by faith, by believing God's Word. You are His child and He is your Father. God is poised and ready to baptize you in His Holy Spirit when you ask Him.

Dear Father in Heaven, please fill me with the Holy Spirit. I believe in You and Your son Jesus Christ. I want to be a vessel for You Lord. Please give me Your spirit so I may walk in Your ways. Amen.

Write Your Petition

The last step is to write out your petition to the Lord. The following is an example of a petition taken from Kenneth Copeland Ministries for healing from feeling overwhelmed from being a caregiver:

Be it known this day, _____, at _____ (a.m./p.m.), that I received healing from the overwhelming feeling of a troubled heart in my body. No negativity of any kind has a place in my body. So, Father in Heaven, in the Name of Jesus, I come boldly to the throne of grace and present Your Word.

According to John 16:23, Jesus said You will grant whatever I ask in His Name. In Mark 11:24, You said whatever I ask in prayer, believing I will receive it, will be given to me.

I declare, according to Isaiah 53:5; Psalm 103:2–5; Psalm 91:9–10,14–16; and 1 Peter 2:24, that Jesus took all of the burden of my caregiving, tomorrow and forever. I am healed by the blood of the Lamb, and I am protected from all physical and mental anguish. I am redeemed from the curse of the law, which includes sickness and disease of any kind (Galatians 3:13).

I bind Satan and all his forces according to Matthew 18:18 and declare they will not hinder me from receiving this promise (Hebrews 1:13–14) and charge them to go forth and cause mercy to come into my hands.

I believe in my heart and declare with my mouth that I AM HEALED. I thank You and praise You for healing me of _____, and I thank You for making me whole.

I believe I received the healing today. I will not waver or doubt at Your promise but will stand firm. I praise You and thank You that I am not waiting for this to manifest—I take it right now and hold it in my spiritual hands.

Signature _____

Date _____

Read and pray your prayer of petition out loud. Have confidence knowing God heard your petition and that is already done. Praise God for His answer to you, that He heard your cry and that already things have shifted in your favor. You will be validated through Christ. You will embark on a new journey as a caregiver.[1]

Come to the Father

In the beginning of my caretaking years, I was young and inexperienced and making decisions by the seat of my pants. American self-help author and motivational speaker, Wayne Dyer, used to say, "There's a spiritual solution to every problem," and I agree with that statement. I agree because not all answers come in the form of action. Sometimes surrendering to your situation and accepting that your loved one has this illness is needed. Along with surrender, I challenge you to go a step further into faith—handing it over to the Lord, giving Him

---

[1] Copeland, K. (n.d.). *How to pray the prayer of petition*. Kenneth Copeland Ministries. https://www.kcm.org/real-help/prayer/learn/how-pray-the-prayer-petition

the power to make do with what He will. Then things move along better at a faster pace. More healing can get done.

Along with healing for your loved one comes healing for yourself. You will start to heal when you notice God is taking care of all your needs and He is creating space for you to live the life He wants you to live.

"As a mother comforts her child, so will I comfort you; and you will be comforted over Jerusalem. When you see this, your heart will rejoice and you will flourish like grass." – Isaiah 66:13–14

When God gave you the responsibility to look after one of His children, He didn't take that lightly. He knows the situation, and He knows how His children suffer. He appointed you the blessing and honor of looking after another person. It is a great commission, it is a calling. Sometimes we are called to do something when we are not ready or developed to do it yet. But God is working on us. He is refining us, challenging us, and moving us. Have you ever noticed that the struggles of your care are followed by great blessing? If you haven't ran away from your responsibilities, if you've accepted the challenge, if you are willing to be a friend and motivator to someone special in your life ... then you will be blessed greatly and rewarded tenfold. That is not to say you won't find challenges or that it will come easy.

In order to learn the lessons quickly, to receive the blessings quickly, you must be in regular contact with the Father. I start my day with rising early, admiring the sunrise, making a cup of coffee, and meeting my devotional and Bible. I also have a notebook where I write down Bible verses that speak to me. They feed me, and they are my armor; they keep me safe and protected.

When I think of a friend or family member who is struggling, I write down in my notebook, "Lord I pray for Christy. Give her peace and comfort Lord as she is feeling overwhelmed by her mother's aging and decline. Let her know she's loved and protected, give her strength." I love praying over my friends and family because I know it's doing so much more than sending a gift in the mail or picking up the phone. I still try to do those things, but it is nothing compared to bringing that person to the altar of the Lord. When you pray for someone, you are spiritually bringing them to the Lord. If they are open to receiving God's blessings, they will benefit immediately from the prayer.

I have witnessed firsthand the power of prayer. I know sick patients who needed surgery and after fervent prayer, the surgeon discovered no surgery was necessary. I have witnessed direct healing for my aunt, my mother's sister, who also suffers daily with depression, to find small comfort from the morning prayers my girls and I recite daily during our Bible time for homeschool. The Lord is near you when you pray. When you pray for others, you are also indirectly praying for yourself. You are laying yourself down at Jesus's feet. You are submitting to Him and saying, "Lord, I know you can handle this and I cannot. Thank You for Your love, and I praise You!" Oh how happy this makes the Lord. And you. We all need support in our lives.

You are LOVED by the Lord. He is your Father. He knit you carefully in the womb. He made you His. He knows every hair on the top of your head. He knows all your pain, your struggles, and your heartache. And when you come to Him, He covers you with His kisses and much anticipation. He craves for you to come to Him. Like every relationship on this earth, we have an intimate relationship with the Lord. It is the most intimate relationship you can possibly have! No one loves you more, cares for you more, and worries for you more than the Lord. There are endless Bible verses about God's love; the most profound one for me is Romans 8:37–39 that says:

"No, in all these things we are more than conquerors through him who loved us. For I am sure that neither death nor life, nor angels nor rulers, nor things present nor things to come, nor powers, nor height nor depth, nor anything else in all creation, will be able to separate us from the love of God in Christ Jesus our Lord."

No one thing will ever be successful in separating us from our father. He loves us so much that He makes this promise to us that He will never leave us. He will never abandon us like so many earthly fathers have done to their sons and daughters. He will always be with us because our relationship is so powerful and so important to Him that nothing can separate us from Him. When I realized that in my own life, I stopped making decisions by the seat of my pants. Instead, I got down on my knees and said, "Lord, I don't know what to do. Help me to make the right decisions for my mom. Help me to see what is in Your will for her. I will do whatever You ask of me, big or small." Then after I said that prayer, I became comforted by the Holy Spirit. I may have still felt some anxiety, I may have wanted a quick answer, but over time and in God's time, I got my answer. I moved forward. I made a decision. It's a beautiful process. Sometimes I look back and I remember my time before the Lord made decisions in my life and I wonder how the heck I even got anything done! God creates so many miracles big and small, and He is the most capable one to turn to. By coming to the Father, you are covered in His favor. You can and will set out to do the things God wants you to do. You will be blessed.

Questions:

1. What lies has Satan tried to fool you into believing about you and about your caregiving?

2. How has your suffering led to something good in your life?

3. What is your biggest struggle right now? How did the Bible verse you found help reassure you God is working to heal you?

Grace

Chapter 2
ALLOWING GOD TO BUILD YOU UP

"And from far away the Lord appeared to his people and said, 'I love you people with a love that will last forever. That is why I have continued showing you kindness. People of Israel, I will build you up again, and you will be rebuilt. You will pick up your tambourines again and dance with those who are joyful.'"

–Jeremiah 31:3-4 NCV

I was eight years old when my mom and I first got kicked out of a Burger King. She was there with her friend Emily and they each had ordered a medium sized Diet Coke and sat down at the table. For six hours. After it became apparent to the manager that they weren't going to be purchasing any French fries, they were kindly asked to leave. Two hours before then, I had been making pretend tacos out of the napkins found at the serving station. My mom had given me a water cup and after filling it about twenty times, I decided to use straws to make an invention out of a plethora of napkins. Then using grey salt and pepper shakers on the table, I seasoned the log of wet napkins to make my delicious and well-seasoned appetizer. This is what kids do when they are bored out of their minds. Let me remind you this was before cell phones and iPads.

Emily weighed 300 pounds and had a thick German accent. She was divorced with one son, who didn't live with her because of her mental problems. My mom and Emily were best friends and had met at the halfway house they both lived in while recovering from mental breakdowns. Often mistaken for lesbians, both lived in the same apartment building for low income disabled folks. I always pictured them like Danny Devito and Arnold Schwarzenegger in the movie *Twins*. My mom was super skinny like a tooth pick and Emily was round and short. They were two peas in a pod.

My mom would bounce a knee nonstop (side effect from psych meds). One time, Emily laughed so hard she peed her pants. It was mortifying to me at the time. I wanted to have a cool mom that looked like other moms. Instead, my mom took a black eyeliner pencil and drew two arrow-like Beavis and Butt-Head eyebrows on top of her naturally blonde hairs. She wore very short cut off shorts with black hose underneath the shorts. Her top showed way too much cleavage, and since she was already in her late forties, I felt this was inappropriate for her age. And then to be seen in public with her for several hours at the Burger King ... I prayed no one from school would see us sitting there in the fast food booth. Luckily for me, no one did that day because we got kicked out. Emily drove us back to the apartment. Her car was a mess and smelled like her dog. At least we didn't have to walk like we usually did when Emily wasn't around.

ALLOWING GOD TO BUILD YOU UP

This was about when I started noticing my mom was not like other moms. I had always known she had a "chemical imbalance" because that's what my Aunt Martha told me over Christmas when I was in the first grade. I would repeat this to my friends whenever they asked why my mom doesn't come to PTO meetings or why I didn't live with her. "Chemical imbalance" sounded fancy to me. And of course, my friend listening would pretend like they knew what I was talking about and continue on like no big deal. All the teachers at my school knew this fact about me. Many of them took pity on me, especially when my dad would forget to pick me up after school. Once when I was in the third grade, my dad forgot and a friendly teacher noticed I was still sitting outside on the front entrance steps. She had frosted grey hair and a wide smile. She drove me to my grandma's house because I knew my dad wasn't home. "He's at work. That's where he always is," I told her.

I had started living with my dad the year prior, in the second grade. My parents had separated when I was a baby. My mom had full custody of me up until the second grade when I moved in with my dad. We lived in an apartment on the shady side of town. He was a small business owner and self-made. He saved every penny only to build what my mother later said was her dream home. My mother was not too pleased. A 3,000 sq. ft. lake house on Lake Winnebago, it had grey carpet everywhere and large bay windows. My mom said she always wanted a house with grey carpet. Then she would call my dad a bastard in a sweet low voice. This rags to riches feeling I was living was lonely and scary. I was used to living with my mom who was loving, caring, and compassionate. She never raised her voice. My dad did raise his voice, on the other hand, and was all about business. He ran a tight ship.

I secretly wanted to go back to the days when I lived with my mom and life was kinder.

I couldn't go back to my mom's house because she was now living at Winnebago Mental Health Institute. I didn't understand what that was at the time. I now understand it to be one of the oldest psych hospitals that today reminds me of a large dusty and green prison. Straight out of a horror movie, my beautiful mama was undergoing shock therapy and Clozaril cocktails in attempts to get her out of psychosis. Once I recall visiting her at Winnebago. She was raging down the hallway with her hair standing straight up. I thought something was really wrong. She must have stuck her finger in a light socket. (My mother always warned me not to do that.) She was singing "Jingle Bells," and it was in the middle of summer. Then when she saw me, she burst into tears. The visit was over, and in an attempt to smooth things over, I was put into a horse and buggy carriage and driven around the hospital grounds. It was the strangest day of my life.

The saddest part of this memory was it was totally blocked out until this year when I turned 38 years old. I was vacationing with my husband and children at Mackinac Island, MI. We rode in a beautiful horse and carriage. That night, I had a dream I was speaking at a conference for promoting awareness of mental health in our country. I was nervous because I was speaking in front of a large crowd. Palms sweating, I clenched the podium and opened up a sheet of paper where I had scribbled some notes down. I cleared my throat and began, "The first time I visited my mom at Winnebago Mental Health Institute I was seven years old ..." I woke up immediately in our hotel room in a sweat. Was I really seven years old the first time I went to Winnebago? Then like pictures out of a movie, it came back to me. A lost picture movie stored dark and deep in the back of my mind. Too scary to unravel. I called my dad that morning and asked him why he took me at such a young age to see my mom in that mental hospital. He told me he didn't take me. Guess what—still to this day I don't know how or why I got there.

Knowing When to Act

It's easy to make decisions for yourself. But what does it look like when you have to make vital decisions on behalf of someone you love? The number one challenge in finding balance for a caretaker is knowing when to step in on behalf of someone else. In life, you should strive for all individuals to live as independent and free as possible. In my mom's case, she suffered with a severe mental disability that took away her decision-making capability to the extremes. She struggled with knowing how to take care of herself because she was so overwhelmed with simple everyday functions that you and I take for granted. An example of this can be found in her personal diary that she kept while I was a teenager. She wrote consistently of how she got lost inside her own apartment. When she couldn't find her keys, she said she would "lose it." She was so impaired that paying bills seemed like climbing Mount Everest.

From my mom's diary: *Still Sunday the 30th, "I could have I should have, did have but I didn't have ... I know know I know know—right then I knew that pair of pants I lost in my apartment were gone forever. So now I only have one pair of pants to wear casual. Did you see how many pairs of jeans with the sizes are at Goodwill by Warehouse Food? And I was worried I'd get lost—no—Did I ever tell you how many* *times I got lost in my own apartment and then panicked at least six times now to make it seven my lucky number and I said maybe my lucky number 9–27 my birthday right."*

There were periods in my mom's life when she was able to make decisions for herself. She had cycles of good mental health. She would keep her apartment clean, go to coffee with a friend, and enjoy shopping in the afternoon. She would cook healthy meals and take omega 3 supplements and enjoy going for walks. But like all cycles, what goes up must come down. Her good luck would come to an end. Slowly she would move inward and isolate herself from her friends. Her apartment would get messy, and she would start to give up the shopping trips she so much enjoyed.

During her downward cycles, regular self-care, like going to the dentist or medical check-ups, were thrown out the window. She could not process in her brain and organize her life in a way that she could make positive decisions for herself. When she stopped going to the dentist because "she didn't believe in dental cleanings anymore," her teeth rotted one after the other. I would try to help her get to the dentist, but she refused. This is when I had to ask myself, "Is she safe?" The answer was no, because if she got an abscess in her mouth, it could go to her heart. It could lead to a lot of pain or worse conditions.

So I did what any loving child would do for her mother. I found a dentist who would pull out all of her teeth in a day and give her dentures. Like forcing her into assisted living without having a say, I tricked her into thinking she was getting her teeth cleaned, when instead they hooked her up to laughing gas and put her to sleep to pull out all her teeth. When she woke up, she asked if we could go to breakfast with blood dribbling down her chin. She had no idea what just happened, and I had a very long car ride with her to her home to explain it all. She didn't talk to me for three months.

Still to this day, I feel such tremendous guilt from having to do this to her, I can't explain it. It's been 15 years and she still asks regularly to get her teeth "permanently implanted" because she doesn't like her dentures. And my heart absolutely breaks for her. I know it was the right thing to do at the time, and I know the dentures now are a pain for her. I have to live with this guilt of having to make a tough decision on my mother's behalf. There are no books that tell you to do what I did. Probably not a professional in the world will tell you to trick your mother and get all her teeth pulled out. I know it took crazy ambition to do it, and I will always carry guilt of some degree about the decision.

Had my mother just agreed to continue to get care for her teeth and regularly go to the dentist, we might still have faced the ultimate decision of getting her dentures anyway; you just never know. Most people eventually in their old age need them. The fact I had to do it so early for her was and still is difficult for both my mother and me. I look at my own smile in the mirror and think how important my teeth are to me. It really hurts knowing I had to make that decision and I had to make the decision for my mom, the person who loves me the most in this world.

In the end, even though it broke my heart, I know I made the right decision for her health. It was early in my guardianship, and looking back, I could have waited until her pain settled in, until she couldn't take it anymore and she herself would make the decision to go to the dentist. I was so proactive and so young and impatient that I pushed forward with a "take charge" mentality. If I could go back and redo it, I honestly do not know what I would do.

Am I Safe, Are They Safe?

There may be times in your life when you will have to make a tough choice for someone else. You need to know when to act and when not to act. This is easier said than done. My answer to that question is always, "Am I safe, are they safe?" If under the current circumstances you can attest to another person's safety, then you know that person is where they need to be. If they are NOT safe, you must act. If YOU are not safe, then you must act. All humans have the basic necessity for safety. We all have the freedom and right to live in a clean and safe environment and know when we put our heads down on the pillow at night that we are well taken care of. Whatever that looks like to you, that is your fundamental right.

Sometimes there are grey areas. In my mom's case, you could argue for both ways—wait and see what kind of pain and complications develop and let her decide, or move forward and take action before the risk sets in. A lot may have to do with your own personality as a caretaker. Whatever it is, make the decision and own it. You will have to pick your battles, and it's very important that you pick the important ones to take a stance on. Like they say, you have to choose carefully what hill to die on.

Have you ever watched Cesar Milan the Dog Whisperer? He is the charismatic dog trainer on TV who shows people how to train the most vicious dogs to be an obedient man's best friend. I like Cesar because he teaches people how to be loving but firm. That is something I myself had to learn over the years. I was afraid to set boundaries with my mom because I loved her and wanted to please her. But by not establishing boundaries with her right away, she learned she could manipulate me into getting what she wanted.

For example, when I didn't draw the line and say, "Mom I will not take you shopping until you get your blood drawn first," she would insist on a shopping trip to Kohl's first and then refuse to get out of the car once we pulled into the clinic. "Mom, c'mon let's get your blood draw done. I'm tired and I have to still get home and cook supper." "NO! I hate blood draws. They give me wrinkles on my arm!" She'd protest. Eventually I would coerce her to go, but it would be a major headache and it would take up extra time for myself. It's always best to first set the boundary lines and be upfront and honest with your loved one. You might even have to tell them no! It's okay. Real and honest love sometimes requires tough love. If you take anything from this book, its permission from me to you to say no to your loved one when you need to. Then you can pray for them and pray for yourself. Pray for understanding and pray for God to reveal to you what is best in every decision.

When You Make a Mistake

When you make a mistake, and trust me you will, you will need to apologize and then let it go. Move on and let go of any of the guilt you have had. I made so many mistakes with my mom and with myself it isn't funny. But then I learned from them. I was quicker and smarter the second time around. You will be too. After I pulled my mom's teeth out and she was angry with me, I told her I was so sorry. And I was! I was sorry I had to make that decision and still to this day carry regret over it.

Forgiveness is a powerful thing. When you are quick to forgive yourself, you are also quick to forgive others. Jesus taught us how to forgive our enemies. If we must forgive our enemies, think of how we should treat ourselves when we do wrong! We must offer grace like Jesus offered grace. If we live inside the guilt, we are submitting to the darkness and not living life in joy. Guilt robs us of our joy and cripples us into submission.

If you've ever been faced with such tremendous guilt that you can't get out of bed or face the very thing that's instilling fear, then you know it is out of hand and something must be done. Satan loves to feed us with guilt because if he convinces us that we are the perpetrators, he can dupe us into thinking we are better off to just run away. That's why many caretakers will throw in the towel. They will let someone else pick up the pieces. They will check out. Don't let it get so bad that you come to a place where you need to escape. If you set up the proper boundaries, if you let go of the guilt, you will be a much happier caretaker and you will not feel the burden so many feel. You will sleep good at night knowing you are doing your best.

Practicing Good Self Care

The last point and perhaps the most overlooked one of building balance in your life as a caretaker is putting in the habit of taking care of yourself first. In the beginning of my walk with my mom, I was so focused on her care and her future that I completely dismissed my own. Luckily, I still had God's protection over me to help me anyway. And so do you! Our God is so good and so loving that He already knows what we need. He is creating miracles for you without you even realizing it. He already has moved mountains for you. He sees that you are tired and weary. He wants you to come to Him and to rest. You cannot be everything to someone. You cannot fulfil another person's complete needs. But Christ can! He can provide perfect loving and perfect protection.

When I moved away from the concept of being everything to my mom, I started to put the Lord first in my life. I went to church on Sundays with my soon-to-be husband, Matthew. My faith didn't click overnight. It grew and it developed over years of time, even decades. By the time I was a young adult in my 30's, I decided to start reading my Bible and getting involved in more Bible studies. When I went, I was reminded that God is in control. And for someone who was such a control freak like myself, it relieved me and calmed me like nothing I had ever experienced before! It took the weight off my shoulders. I could hear God whispering to me that I had done my best, but I was not operating at the level He wanted me to. God saw how tired I was and He wanted me to find comfort in His arms. And I did.

The Bible says in Psalm 119:165 that those who love the Lord's instructions have great peace and do not stumble. In other words, if you love the Lord and what He asks of you, if you follow His commandments, the simple rules that we all know (love our neighbors, love our enemies, do not steal or kill, do not compare and become jealous of your neighbor), we will desire the Lord over everything else. When our hearts are set on Him, our minds become balanced and the weight of caretaking is not as heavy as it once was, because we know who's in control. We know that our source of peace comes from the Father, not from the personal achievements we are making in our lives or with our caretaking.

The most important step of self-care is relieving yourself of the burden and thought that you have to have it all together. If we don't ask for help, if we don't seek the Lord, if we don't seek the help from others, we are trapped in our reality of living in the "less than" deficit. It's a lonely place to be. In this place, Satan can have the power to try and convince you that you are the only one going through this, that you are failing, and that God doesn't see your pain. These are the deepest and darkest lies that I at one time believed, and I am thankful that today I know they are all lies that Satan used to put me down.

When I realized God was in control, that I could step away from my mom for a little bit, that I could do something at this very moment to make me happy, it was a freeing thought. At first, I didn't even know what I needed. I was so conditioned to put others before myself that I didn't know how to ask for myself. I started praying to God, "Show me what I need Lord." In a matter of hours, I knew that I had to start putting my health as a priority.

I started seeing a specialist for my migraines that lead me to getting my teeth reshaped to help lessen my TMJ. I got massages and sought talk therapy so I had a professional that understood what I was going through in my life as a primary caretaker for my mom. I invested in myself. And the dividends paid off. I started sleeping better at night. I didn't lie awake with anxiety, because I was doing the work during the day to help myself. I kept a journal during the day to let out all my fears and worries, related to my mom or not, and it helped me sleep better at night. I continued my Bible study and reading and believing God's promises of restoration for me. It healed me and continues to heal me to this day.

Ways You Can Love Yourself:

1. Go on nature walks.
2. Read a good book on a subject you enjoy.
3. Get a manicure/pedicure.
4. Get a massage.
5. Go to the movies.
6. Take up a new hobby.
7. Sign up for a marathon.
8. Adopt a pet from the humane society.
9. Take a self-defense class.
10. Start a small Bible study.

Do You Love Yourself?

What does it look like to love yourself? *Really* love yourself? I think it's so easy to just set your own needs aside and go through the motions. Yesterday morning, my kids were all hungry for breakfast and I realized in a panic we were out of butter and my eyes were crusty from sleep and the dogs were hungry and I stumbled around and heated up some oatmeal in the Instant Pot—but all of a sudden, the machine had a *burn* alert. I unplugged it and used an oven mitt to pull the bowl and its contents out, put the oats in a new pan on the stove, and prayed it would still cook okay. The dogs were following my every step, so I quickly fed them before feeding the kids mushy oatmeal with maple syrup on top. I hoped they wouldn't notice. I poured myself a cup of coffee and grabbed my morning devotional, Bible, and journal. As I started to read, I felt my pulse slow down and my breathing calm. The kids were happily eating their mush and the dogs were satisfied. As I slipped into a conversation with the Lord, as I thanked Him for another crazy morning... I started to feel my own stomach grumble.

I finished my prayers and closed the books. One of the kids asked me to approve an app download on her iPad. "No, not now." I replied. Mama needs fuel. I kindly said, "Unless you want me to eat *you* for breakfast, please give me some space so I can eat." The kids are old enough to understand this and they immediately carried on to their next adventure—an art project, a book, or morning cartoons. I'm not going to lie, I felt a tiny bit guilty. I probably sounded grumpy and I wasn't totally present with them or responsive because I was just responding to the day. But I needed to feed myself so I would have the energy later to play with my kids, prepare lunch, take the dogs for a walk, etc. Since when was it bad to take care of yourself? Where did I get that idea from? God tells us in the Bible to be kind to ourselves first and then extend kindness to others. "Let each of you look not only to his own needs, but also to the interest of others" (Philippians 2:4 ESV). Notice it doesn't say to only look after others, it says in the first part to look after your own needs, then following the comma it says to look after others.

Growing up, I learned to put myself down. I saw my friends do it, I saw my cousins do it, even my own mother put herself down constantly. We live in a culture where it's acceptable to be melancholy. Don't! Don't fall for the ways of the world (1John 2:15). Follow God's commandments and rest in His promises. God is very clear about the number one way for you to practice self-care, and that is by coming to Him. "Come to me, all who labor and are heavy laden, and I will give you rest" (Matthew 11:28). He also wants us to be joyful and a happy giver (2 Corinthians 9:7).

Provide a Legacy of Love

Don't hesitate today to create a legacy of love. What exactly does that mean? What do you want to be remembered for on this earth? We all one day expire and go to the Lord. Others will only have our memories to keep them warm. Do you believe you've created warm memories for others to cherish? Did you provide good care to others? Did you also extend that warmth to yourself? If you don't feel like you've done a good job with that, well welcome to the club! It's never too late to change or make small steps towards creating that legacy.

So many people talk about financial legacy. My husband and I have a financial planner that talks to us about investing now so we can leave a legacy to our kids later. We laugh because we want to enjoy our money and also give our money freely away. We don't want to leave our kids that kind of a legacy! Instead, we want to leave them a legacy of love. We want them to have picture books filled with places we've traveled together, recipes we cooked together, jokes we laughed over together, and even restaurants we've dine together at. The small stuff matters! We want our kids and our family and friends to have those memories of us.

Why not make memories today with the people you care about? Do you have family or friends that you've been setting aside because you're too busy attending care conferences, talking to doctors, or afraid to travel because you're worried of leaving behind those that aren't well enough to travel along with you? It's time to stop that. You need to let go of the guilt.

It was Easter 2019 and my mom was really sick. She was put on hospice and we thought maybe she was going to pass away soon. We had plane tickets to travel to the southwest to see family. We were looking forward to golfing and swimming in the pool and just that getaway. But deep in my heart I felt terrible for leaving behind my mother. Thankfully, after sitting in prayer and getting quiet, I heard God tell me life is meant to be lived! That if my mom were well she would want me to go! So I went. I called every day to check on her and she did just fine. I had a wonderful break and I can't tell you how much more I was ready to be at my mother's side after we returned from abundant sunshine.

Go outside of your comfort zone. Take more trips. Visit other countries and cultures. Sometimes just taking an hour-long drive is enough to get a whole new change of scenery and you might find a cute little diner you've never noticed before. Stop and enjoy it. Treat your friend to a supper club meal. Have a grasshopper. Visit a local winery. Go to your local farmers market and try homemade jam. Treat yourself. By doing this, you will be more present. You will notice things around you. Stop doing the same old thing over and over again because it's comfortable. Take a chance and see what new adventure is waiting for you.

ALLOWING GOD TO BUILD YOU UP

Stop and smell the roses. When you have a second, and you are admiring God's nature, ask Him to make it clear what He wants you to do next. Then don't hesitate to take that leap. It's only in the quiet and content that we are able to hear that voice of clarity. Now is your time to tap into that source of comfort.

Questions:

1. If you had all the money in the world, what would you do? How has your caregiving gotten in the way? Is it too late?

2. Are you safe? Is your loved one safe? Why or why not?

3. Is there anything you need to do for your loved one on their behalf? Is there something scary or difficult to face that you've been putting off?

Dear Lord,

I carry many heavy burdens while taking care of my loved one. Help me to see when to step in on their behalf. Help me to make good decisions for them and for me. Help me to start doing the things I love again. Help me to make my personal goals.

Thank You, Lord! In Your Name I pray!

Surrender

Chapter 3
LET GO AND LET GOD

"My flesh and my heart fail; But God is the strength of my heart and my portion forever."

–Psalm 73:26 NKJV

I have never experienced more tenderness than from my mother. While I have seen her get worked up and upset, I've even seen her in fits while under psychosis, which is very scary to witness, this is not what I'm talking about. Her general temperament while treated for her Schizophrenia is something I've admired all my life. Simply she is funny, witty, and downright supportive. She doesn't judge a single person. How can she? She knows she isn't perfect. She used to have a wooden knick knack on the top of her TV. It was several nuts in a row and below it had a sign that said, "We're all a little nuts." My mom had such a great sense of humor!

I'm going to try and give you an example of what my mother was like during her good years. I recall as a child when she used to talk to her girlfriends on the phone for hours. She didn't have to work a fulltime job all day like many other moms did because of her illness. Most days it was hard enough for her to get dressed, find the keys of her apartment, venture outside for a walk, and prepare meals for herself. These everyday things were enough for her to focus on. When she was on the phone, she would listen intently to her sister or friends who would call. She would say "uh huh" five hundred times. I used to get really irritated with her. Why does she say "uh huh" over and over again? What is the point? But my mom was listening with great interest. She had this way about her for being compassionate towards others. She knew what to say and when to say it. When she said "Oh no," it was so low and honest. When she laughed out of humor, she tilted her head all the way back and let out a bellow so high pitched and funny you couldn't help but laugh out loud with her! I truly think my mom invented the concept of LOL.

Her sincerity was real. She felt pain when you felt pain. She was greatly concerned about me as a kid. Maybe a little overprotective but there's no such thing from the viewpoint of a child. A child always wants to be fawned over and loved on and fussed over. That never got old for me. She used to worry about strangers kidnapping me. One time when I was a baby, she took me out to lunch and the waitstaff at the restaurant asked if they could take me back to the kitchen to show me off (I was that beautiful of a baby apparently!). She kindly agreed, only to feel extremely scared once I was whisked away out of her sight. Can you imagine? I remember hearing this story and the storyteller was almost laughing about the fact my mom believed I had been kidnapped. What new mother wouldn't feel that way?

Sometimes I don't think the symptoms of Schizophrenia are really that off base from normal feelings we all feel. They are just accelerated. Under medication, most

Schizophrenic patients are loving, tender, compassionate, kind, funny, and loyal. They understand suffering. You have the wonderful opportunity of knowing someone affected by Schizophrenia. Make it a point in your life to befriend them. Walk with them. Listen to them, and let them listen to you. My mom had many friends and many beautiful relationships in her life. In fact, that is something I will always try to strive for. Am I as good of a friend as my mother was? Do I listen with tenderness? Do I treat my family the same? The people I love the most, do I always have time and energy for them? These are really good questions to ask yourself regularly.

I have to mention here, I believe my mom was so tender because of her faith in Christ. I also believe that is how she is still living today. Without her faith in love, promises, and support from her God, I do not believe she would be able to turn it over to others. There's no other way to make it through years of psych hospital stays, shock treatments, and medications that make her hands tremble and thinking that goes foggy. For most of her young life and into her 70's, my mom maintained a vitality of life. She loved brisk walks in the winter time only to come home to a baked potato in the oven. She enjoyed cooking simply and healthfully. She looked forward to silence and naps on her couch. She rarely complained about anything. Ever. And occasionally she had a good cry. She always told me, "Becky never underestimated the power of a good cry. We, as humans, need to get it out." I remember her crying was quiet and steady. Even her crying was that of an angel.

How to Have a Good Cry

How to have a good cry: (this is especially effective during the holidays!) Remember CASTLE. A castle is strong and protective. It keeps our soul safe and cleanses any bad thoughts or vibes. Crying is not a sign of weakness. It's a powerful and effective tool to create self-awareness and encourage positivity into your life. We cannot fill in goodness into our bodies if we are filled with sadness inside. Like a filthy house, we must first clean it and declutter it before decorating.

Cas·tle

/ˈkasəl/

noun

- 1. a large building, typically of the medieval period, fortified against attack with thick walls, battlements, towers, and in many cases, a moat

1. C—is for Clothes. Put comfy clothes on that are soft and familiar. Old pajamas always do the trick.

2. A—is for Ambience. Put on some soft music. Lower the lights if it's night time. My mother always used to like having twinkling Christmas lights.

3. S—is for Sit. Sit on the couch and breathe. If you want to sit in the fetal position with arms wrapped around your legs, go ahead.

4. T—is for Think. Think about what is hurting you. Don't turn away from it. Turn towards it.

5. L—is for Letting it go. As your emotions heighten, allow those thoughts to come and go. If your body releases and allows you to, don't fight the tears. Let it roll.

6. E—is for Escape. After you feel all of your emotions have escaped your body, blow your nose and curl up under a blanket. Sigh and let out a smile. You've just done yourself a big favor of allowing your emotions to be validated.

Being validated in our emotions is very important. Whether your fears are real or irrational does not matter. Have you ever noticed that life is just an experience of emotions? No one on their deathbed names off all the

UNBINDING *Love*

facts they learned in school. No one remembers facts. But emotions, experiences, even jokes, now those are memorable because of how they made us *feel*. God created our bodies to experience emotion. How wonderful and merciful that He did that for us!

Questions:

1. When was the last time you had a good cry? Did it help?

2. Many people mistakenly believe crying to be an indication of weakness. What would you tell them?

3. What have you been feeling emotional about? What is God telling you?

Perception Is Key

"Let us acknowledge the Lord; let us press on to acknowledge him. As surely as the sun rises, he will appear; he will come to us like the winter rains, like the spring rains that water the earth."

–Hosea 6:3 NIV

My youngest daughter Julie and I went to visit Mom on a Tuesday morning in the winter of 2019. At first, the day started off like every other normal day until the girls noticed a bug on our dog Minnie's belly. "Ew, get it off!" But the harder they tried, they couldn't get the tiny black bug out of her fur. I came into the room carrying a small Ziplock bag. Somehow, I rubbed the bug out and into the soon to be insect coffin. I secured the teeny tiny bug into detention, checked for other bugs, and sighed with relief when none were found. "Does Minnie have fleas you think?" The kids asked. My stomach felt sick. I really hoped it wasn't a flea.

That's what led me into Winston, the town where my mom lives in her nursing home. I went to the vet to have them examine the teeny tiny black bug just so they could tell me it was a flea. Since I was in Mom's neck of the woods, Julie and I decided to hop over to the nursing home to see how she was that day. I hadn't visited for about ten days because Julie had strep throat. I didn't want to share any germs with her. For those ten days, I called almost every day because I knew that she was mentally not good. My mom today is 76 years old and dementia has set in. Her brain is like a radio station that comes in and out.

Perception. Here is where perception becomes important. If I picture my mom at her best, like around her birthday time when she was walking and talking and able to feed herself, then I'm set up for disappointment right off the bat. If I think of her lowest low, when she was on hospice and taking in regular doses of Morphine, whatever she will be today will give me great joy. You would think I would just always be able to keep a low standard and expect nothing from her so that I was always pleasantly surprised. But the truth is I can't do that!

Sometimes when I visit, I'm on one side and other times I'm at the other. I flip flop between hopeful and dreadful. It's just the way it is. I think that's okay. Don't we need to have one emotion to have the other? We cannot experience pure joy if we don't experience pure hell. There is no black without white. No peace without war. No justice without injustice. So, what does that mean? Am I suggesting we need the bad side of things? Yes. We do. We need to suffer once in a while so that we can rejoice in the healing.

God brings us healing. He brings us the calm after the storm. He is behind every healing and everything that's free. Because He is pure love, that is all He is capable of. Healing, loving, hoping, wishing over His children. When I see my mom laying on the medical bed, hair a wild mess, food dribbling out of the corners of her mouth, eyes cloudy, I try to look at her like Christ would look at her. Pure love. Pure acceptance. It isn't easy. You want to take a rag and wipe her mouth clean. You want to ask for help, ask for more medication to ease her pain, ask for anything, maybe a fresh pillowcase. But the reality is nothing can really change what's happening on the inside. As my mom draws closer to death, so does her suffering. It's a difficult, slow, up and down approach, and to be at her side as her witness is at times excruciating.

Yet through this season of winter (as I speak there is snow outside on the ground but it is also winter inside my mother's body), it seems all of life has frozen up, all the beautiful flowers and green grass has withered away, leaving an atmosphere so barren and bleak that you're not sure if you can find any beauty in the cold season. But I'm here to tell you ... you can! Have you ever seen a picture of the winter snow that was so fresh and clean and bright and white that just looking at the scenery gave you a sense of cleanliness and peace? Picture the woods at Christmas time, with deep mounds of snow and a little bunny rabbit poking its nose through the drifts. Deep red berries are poking out through the snow and there is life amongst the winter!

This is what you feel like while your loved one is in their winter season. Maybe they are in hospice and they are shifting in and out of reality. Your control over what's happening to them slips away. Your desire to change things for them is no longer because you know there is a higher power working. The Lord is calling His child home. It is a very difficult and yet awe-inspiring transition. This season of winter as I call it, is a season that requires patience, faith, love, and surrender. The surrendering part is the last and most profound part.

How do we get to a place of surrender? How do we stretch our arms wide and call on the Lord Almighty? How do we let go of someone who is so dear to us? How is it possible? It's not really a question because there really is no one perfect answer.

I think I am still stuck inside that question to be perfectly honest.

I don't think it's ever possible to really let go of a loved one. But I do think it's possible to surrender. Let's go over the difference between the two. The first suggestion of letting go of a loved one is simply not possible. Even after we physically lose someone who was close to us, we still have the memories, lots of physical reminders that they were once here on earth. Sometimes it's a smell that takes us back to them. My grandmother's skin used to have a sweet scent, and sometimes when I'm outside walking or shopping, I can smell her on my own skin. She used to make me the best BLTs for lunch when I was a child. Now when I take a bite of a BLT, my heart swells with the reminder of her love. It's that simple. That will never go away.

Surrendering is much more profound because in order to surrender, we must actively take a step of faith. What I mean by that is we must close our eyes, our hearts, and our minds to all understanding and hand it over to a higher power. In my life, I know I need the Lord to take it for me. I know I can't do it all on my own. I know it takes a village to raise a child. I know it takes a village to raise me up! When I can honestly say I know I still need care and love like a child, that is the first step towards having a surrender-like faith. It's humbling and even a little humiliating to admit I'm still a little girl underneath my tough and bold exterior. I look and act like an adult, but deep inside I still need my loving Father God. I still need that nurturing, understanding, and wisdom.

And to be big enough to admit that is a wonderful thing.

When You're in the Rain and Don't Have an Umbrella

Picture you're walking down a busy street. We'll call it the street of life. Picture this street is in NYC and there are crowds of people walking down the street, quickly getting to where they need to go. Some older professionals have their suitcases and high heels; they are intently walking to work. The students all have their backpacks and some are wearing their AirPods and talking on their iPhones. The energy is all the same, everyone has somewhere to go. And so do you.

All of a sudden, thick rain drops start pounding the pavement and you. You look up at the sky and the dark clouds are hovering over you. A low bellow of thunder is heard a few miles away, it's slow cry comes out like an old grandmother telling you to put on your winter coat before playing in the snow. "Warning!" it's saying. The first thing you notice is all the busy professionals pull out their umbrellas. The students even have hoodies conveniently over their heads to protect themselves from the rain. When you notice you don't have a thing but your body, the drops are now making your shirt wet, and you realize something has to happen or you'll soon be like a wet seal at the zoo.

This is how it feels to love someone with Schizophrenia. Stuck. Hopeless. Afraid. Cold. Lonely. Helpless. The list goes on. When you get stuck in the downpour (and it will happen) and you don't have an umbrella (and you won't!), what do you do? Some might run ... they might look for the closest building to safely enter until the storm has subsided. This is good because you're protecting yourself, but bad because now you've had a detour in your plans, and whatever your destination is, it's now waiting for your arrival. Some might run to wherever they need to go, soaking wet, never looking back. This is hard because you've exhausted yourself, you've done it completely alone, and all your energy will be put into surviving that event. Think of your adrenals. Like an Olympic runner, your entire body is stressed and pounding with energy. But many people relate to this, so they will continue to exasperate themselves until they make their goal.

But what if I told you there was a third option? One that didn't exhaust you, didn't make you feel stressed, one that seems silly or strange and even a little bizarre at first. What if I told you to sit in the rain with your arms stretched wide. What should you do then? I have found an alternative when you are in a scary situation with a loved one, and there can be a lot of examples of these situations such as they stopped taking their meds, or they are on medication but not responding to their medication, they are in the hospital, or worse, they are out of their minds but still living on their own, or maybe they are living with you and the burden is too heavy to take. Whatever the situation is, you are in the rain and you don't have an umbrella. You don't have what the other people around you have. If you go to a trusted friend and tell them your situation with your loved one, they won't understand. Chances are they have not been impacted in a direct way from Schizophrenia. There is no way possible for a therapist, friend, or loved one to even remotely understand your pain of loving someone with Schizophrenia. But God does.

God does! God knows. "Okay," you might be thinking. "Yes, so what? How does this help me? I can't hear God. I don't know what He's thinking or wanting me to do. Sometimes I pray at night, and in the end, I just exhaust myself! The only relief is some sleep. When I wake up in the morning, it's the same hopelessness all over again." There is hope in this situation. Let me tell you a profound and crazy tip. Let this be the hacks of all hacks. It's found in Isaiah. God wants us to know this when we are in pain—Stop looking for an umbrella and just look UP.

"Oh, that you would rend the heavens and come down,
that the mountains would tremble before you!
As when fire sets twigs ablaze
and causes water to boil,
come down to make your name known to your enemies
and cause the nations to quake before you!
For when you did awesome things that we did not expect,
you came down, and the mountains trembled before you.
Since ancient times no one has heard,
no ear has perceived,
no eye has seen any God besides you,
who acts on behalf of those who wait for him."

—Isaiah 64:1–4

Do you know who your enemy is in this scripture? The enemy, the darkness, is Schizophrenia. It tries to rob you of joy and your loved one of all their beautiful gifts. When you stop and think of your loved one and what they would be like without mental illness, you know deep in your heart that this condition is the enemy. It kills, steals, and destroys. But what does God say to do? In this scripture, God is reminding us of His true power. He is so big and so powerful that if we were to face Him, He would cause the Earth to tremble. Schizophrenia has nothing on Him!

You walk up to Schizophrenia and you stare it in the face. You say, "Hi this is (enter your name). I'm friends with the Lord. You think you have control, but you don't. You think you can rob my loved one from all, well you can't. I'm here to tell you there's a new boss in town!" You read this scripture and you start to realize the depth of God's power. (We are mere humans and can only understand a teeny tiny bit of His power.) But if you read it, you know it. If you know it, you can believe it.

Okay great, but how do we apply this to my practical situation? This all sounds great, but I'm still in the darkness.

Exactly.

The rain is still coming down and you're still stuck on the busy street without an umbrella. This is the new state of life for you if you love someone with mental illness. There will be a few scattered days when you have your umbrella and you say "PHEW! Close call!" Maybe it was a small problem that found a solution, and you release a HUGE sigh of relief. But as soon as that problem is conquered, another one arises. Ah such is life!

Oftentimes I feel like Schizophrenia is the fast track to continuous problems. Maybe they can't find a social worker they love and then all of a sudden, they are assigned a new one that they can relate to and listen to. You think, "Good! We got over that hurdle." But like many times I've witnessed with my mom, their enthusiasm and hope get crushed within a mere day or so. It doesn't last because there's always new darkness. A fear. A rejection. A nightmare they have over and over. Old demons are hard to shake, and when someone has Schizophrenia, their demons and fears can control everything.

How do you help someone who is so controlled by this fear? How do you help yourself with your own fear? Well, the short answer is YOU CAN'T. You can't. What kind of self-help book is this? "This is crazy," you might be thinking. Yes, all of this is crazy! Crazy your loved one is crazy. Crazy you can't help them. Crazy when you're in a hopeless situation where others really don't get it. And crazy because there is no instant relief, no easy button to speak of.

Just sit in that for a moment. That feeling of panic, that feeling of hopelessness … That's what the enemy wants. I'll say it again. That's what the enemy wants.

"But wait … what? So, you want me just to stop worrying about all of this? Just hand it to the Lord. Jesus take the wheel! Great, well that all sounds dandy, but I'm still in the darkness and I'm scared and I can't get out. I have no frickin' umbrella!"

Hold up! Hold up and look up. This is where you need to change your perception. This is where the magic begins. Because if you can learn to live and sit in the darkness of Schizophrenia, then you can live and sit in anything. ANYTHING! When we get a teeny tiny scratch on our finger and it hurts, we think, "OW!" But when we get in a car accident and we break our legs, we go back to the memory of that teeny tiny scratch on our finger and we think, "Oh I wish it were only a scratch!" That is the power of perception, the power of realizing in each and every setback that this can be tamed. This problem is a problem, but there could always be worse problems. If you can have the attitude and mentality of "hey this is no big deal because I know the Lord. The Lord who causes the earth to shake, who does awesome things, who loves me, who loves my loved one with Schizophrenia" then you have conquered it. You have conquered Schizophrenia. You have told Schizophrenia to take its shame, its sadness, and its ability to steal, and you tell it to go take a HIKE JACK! The day you realize all will be good in a situation that has no good, you have conquered it.

Psychosis

I was sixteen years old and I had just gotten my license. My first vehicle was a 1982 GMC Jimmy with Tasmanian Devil mud flaps on the back that I bought with my own money that I saved over the years. It looked like a dream to me, but to everyone else it was an ugly piece of metal. I'll never forget the feeling of freedom I had the first time I buckled up inside my Jimmy and ventured out on my own. It was the most liberating feeling, and that car, although an eye sore, served me well for the first two years of driving in high school.

My mom had started acting strange, but being young and inexperienced with her mental illness, I didn't know what was happening. It was springtime and the flowers were starting to pop up out of the ground and baby buds of life were sprouting from the branches on trees. Things were waking up outside and things were waking up inside my mother. She hadn't slept in several days. I thought she was less social than usual, and she also said random bizarre comments to me, which was quite usual for her. She would tell me about her romance with the Egg Man and the Indian and how he was going to start taking her to her appointments from now on and I wouldn't need to. She did have one request and that was to drive her to the shopping mall in Fond Du Lac to go to Sears to pick out a new comforter for her bed. As soon as we got into my Jimmy, I knew it was going to be an interesting drive.

She started rhyming a song that sounded like a mix of a bad diapers commercial and "Thriller" from Michael Jackson. The words were garbled and her eyes looked large like saucers. I knew something wasn't right, but I was willing to wing it. My first thought was maybe she'd feel better from the car ride. Like an uncontrollable newborn, I pictured buckling up my mother in the front seat of the car and lulling her back to the life from the country road drive.

As we moved away from the city and turned south on Hwy 21 Fond Du Lac Rd, the many houses we drove past turned to farmland. We escaped the city to a slower paced surrounding. The further away from the city we went, the more ecstatic she became in the car. "BECKY, I COCKED THE COCK. I COCKED THE COCK. SLOW DOWN! GO FAST. I can't do it Becky. The rain came down again. If she says one more thing to me I'm going to really lose it." Then she would close her eyes in an attempt to calm herself or check out for a while, I was not really sure exactly. I thought, "Good. She got that out, let's let her sleep."

I asked her if she was tired. She glared at me like I was a monster out of a Halloween thriller movie. Apparently, that was the wrong thing to say. I shifted in my seat and pretended to look out at something interesting off the road. She was on an electric high. She was nervous, anxious, high flying, terrified, and fed up all in one. If you can imagine taking every feeling you can feel and putting it inside my mother, that is what she was feeling. It was the most uncomfortable thing to witness, and I was trying to focus on the road. I wasn't perfectly comfortable with highway driving yet, so you can imagine my uneasiness.

We never made it to the mall. I still remember turning around on an old driveway right before Hwy 21 comes into Fond Du Lac. It appeared to be a boat landing and had thick greenery just in front of the lake. I stopped and pulled over so I could focus on her and try and calm her down. I realized also that my palms had been sweating like a leaky faucet. To say I was anxious was an understatement. I was completely clueless how to help her. I had never been in this situation before, and I felt responsible for her. I wanted to snap her out of it. Or let her get it out so she could sleep. Or shove her pills down her throat. Whatever I could do I was going to attempt.

Whatever I said or attempted to say didn't do a darn thing. We turned back towards town. We were almost back into city limits when in an attempt to throw herself out of the car, my mom opened her door with the pavement of the cement whizzing by. We were going 60 MPH in my trusty GMC Jimmy and there were no fancy bells and whistles to prevent her from flying out of it. My heart raced. "Mom *what are you doing*!?" I pulled over and safely shut the passenger side door. Then when I got back into the car, I locked all the doors with us safely inside. I thought to myself, "Now I'm going to lose it! We're going to both be crazy inside one vehicle." I knew I had to get her back to her apartment, but it felt like I was driving to the other side of the country. The feeling inside was we were never going to get there.

When we finally arrived, I helped her into her apartment and looked at her bubble pack of pills. Sure enough, the pills were all neatly in a row still placed in her pack. Untouched. My mom had gone off her pills. In exasperation, I popped open the morning pills for today and placed the seven huge pills in my hand. I got a glass of water and approached the couch where my mom was sitting. In a calm voice that I wanted to sound authoritative, but instead said, "Mom, will you please take your pills?" The monster eyes glared back at me. She didn't even say anything back. I thought that meant to go ahead and feed her the pills. Like a baby, I would spoon feed her if I had to. I took the first pill and went for her mouth. As it was half way passed her lips, she bit down like a vulture and that sucker wasn't moving. She shook her head like a wolf eating its prey. She let out a scream like nothing I've heard a human make. And that was when I got out of dodge. I ran away like a scared mouse. I had to get out of that apartment. I was done trying to be her savior.

The next day, I got a call from her landlord. He said she was running down the hallway of her apartment naked. He asked me to call someone. I didn't know who to call! I tried calling Don, my mom's social worker, but it was a Sunday, and he wasn't in his office. So, I called 911. I'll never forget pulling into my mom's apartment and seeing the firetruck, ambulance, and half the Oshkosh police department in the parking lot. My hands started to sweat again. What had I done? This seemed like so much commotion. What would people think?

"Are you Elaine's daughter?" The policeman asked. "Yes," I replied, so embarrassed I wanted to crawl underneath my car and die. "We got about three men right now trying to get your mom out from underneath her bed. She is really putting up a fight. She was threatening to commit suicide, and that's when we stepped in. If she's attempted to harm herself or someone else, we have a right to get her help. Do you understand what I'm saying?" I didn't, but I nodded. I never saw her being carried out by a team of men. I never saw her because sometime during this conversation they got her inside the ambulance. I drove out of that driveway as fast as I could. I couldn't wait to escape the craziness I just witnessed and get back to normal.

There were many other times from my sophomore year until my senior year that I would have to call 911 or her social worker to get her hospitalized. About once or twice a year, my mom would go into psychosis. Sometimes she would go off her meds. Sometimes she would still be taking her meds but she'd still get sick anyway. It seemed that's just what her body wanted to do. And at times, it didn't make sense. At least it didn't make any sense to me.

One time she was getting sick and I called 911. When the ambulance came along with the paramedics, she was able to say her name and what year it was so they said there was nothing they could do and left. She turned to me and called me a lot of names and that was how that ended. Six days later, she ended up face down in a stranger's driveway after running off away from a devil. She had been hallucinating and fell while running too fast. The police found her confused and bloody and that was enough to take her in.

By the time I was a senior in high school, I was beginning to see the pattern of her mental illness and understand it better. I realized I had no real control over it. And that was the first step of processing my mom and her illness. Back in those days, Satan had the power to make me feel such sadness over her condition. I mean I really felt it! I felt as miserable inside as she looked on the outside. I was so new to caretaking and so young I took everything in and made it personal. I made it personal because it was personally messing up my life. Everything that I thought I had control of I really didn't. It made me feel vulnerable, misunderstood, abandoned, and worst of all, damaged goods.

I hated the feeling and would go back to school with my new white tennis shoes on and trick everyone into thinking I was the perfect girl next door. But inside, I knew "the truth," which was actually a lie. The lie was what Satan was telling me. I believed him because I didn't know the Lord well or have a relationship with Him yet. I was raised Catholic and believed you should go to Mass every Sunday. I am not putting down the Catholic faith. I was raised that as long as you went to church on Sunday, that was enough. I didn't know you could have a relationship with Him. Even though I said prayers at night, it wasn't really a working relationship. In fact, I had memorized my evening prayer and recited the same thing every time I prayed:

"Now I lay me down to sleep. I pray the Lord my soul to keep. If I should die before I wake, I pray the Lord my soul to take. Amen. God bless Mommy and Daddy, Grandma and Grandpa, the ones I love, the ones that help me, Father Jackson, Auntie Martha, Carol Smith, and all the others I forgot. Amen."

Father Jackson, Auntie Martha, and Carol Smith were three important people in my mom's life. So, I had memorized the prayer she taught me and then said that prayer the same for 18 years. Can you imagine that?! That was my relationship with the Living God!

You see, I didn't know how to have a relationship with the Lord. I didn't know it was even possible. I pictured God as an old man up in heaven, waving His authoritative staff at me. Maybe even passing judgements on me. I didn't know that He loved me so very much and He was with me while going through what I was going through with my mom. I didn't know that He was crying tears from heaven. I didn't know that He loved me so much He knew every count of hair on my head. I only knew embarrassment and shame. And that led me to a place in my life where the focus became on perfection and being a people pleaser. It was all I could think of to do. And so I put those pants on for a while. And it became a very lonely and relentless lifestyle.

I graduated high school a nervous wreck. I had tried to do everything right for my mom and dad, and yet I couldn't please either one of them. I earned my diploma with honors, and yet inside I felt like a fraud. I was so convinced by the devil that I wasn't really who I let others think I was. I never told my friends all of the stories about my mom because I didn't want them to think I was weird. Everything on the outside mattered to me. It mattered to me because I wasn't looking at how valuable I really was on the inside. I wasn't listening to my Heavenly Father and His invitation to come to Him.

Learning to Let Go of Perfect

That drive for perfection never really went away. If I'm honest, I still fight against it now. Today I am married with kids, I homeschool and work from the house, I have a wonderful support system of loving friends and family. But I am still a caregiver for my mom, and at times I can feel my old self creeping back in trying to grab onto some control.

For so many years, I had been going through the "mission" of taking care of my mom on my own. Along with meeting her needs, I had to raise myself from child to adult. Years down the road, I had to raise my children at the same time of being her guardian and caretaker. At times, I felt and still feel like the world is on my shoulders. I literally go to the masseuse and she tells me my shoulders are like two large boulders. I carry all the weight of the world right there. At times I have to escape. Other days, I'm ready to take on the world. Most days, to be honest, I feel like I'm the only one carrying this burden of being a parent to my parent. Yes, many women my age have children and are living the "rat race," but most of them have parents who are active grandparents to their children, offering babysitting on the weekends or help with preschool pick up and drop off. I'm in so many ways like an orphan.

One thing I want to add here is that I realize I am not an orphan. God gave me two loving parents, and although they are not perfect, they have both done their best with what they were given. The relationship I have with my dad is healing and my understanding today of what I perceived as a child is growing and evolving. God is working and God is so good.

As difficult as it's been taking care of my mom, it's also been one of the most beautiful experiences, because when you actually sit in a tough yoga pose, something more flexible and functional comes out of it. Like any hard-earned lesson or math final, after you've worked and prepared, you can sit in a job well done and know that it really wasn't all you. It was God and Him in that situation, and that one thing that lead to another thing, that lead you to some heartache, some challenge, some disbelief that forced you to get out of your inexperienced corner and seek a new way. When you did, you saw that inside that thing or that person that caused you the sadness, you realized that you too had the same sad thing inside you.

UNBINDING *Love*

That really, when it comes down to it, we are all connected like beads on a string. We are all the same. And I am my mother. That is what 18 years of being her guardian has taught me. This is tough stuff! It's real! And it hurts! But at the end of the pain, the rainbow is that all along she was my mother and she loved me. And no one else on this planet will ever love me more, period.

Questions:

1. What have you been trying to do perfectly in your caregiving that you feel like you're failing at?

2. What would it feel like to let go of that perfection? What would it look like?

3. A well-balanced caregiver cares for himself or herself as well or better than his or her loved one. Do you think that's possible for you? Why or why not?

Dear Lord,

Please help me to let go of the need to be perfect in my caregiving. Help me to see that my needs are just as important as my loved one's with Schizophrenia. I know how much You love me and how important I am to You, but sometimes I forget. Remind me that Your love is enough.

In Your Name I Pray!

"May the Lord direct your hearts to the love of God and to the steadfastness of Christ."

–2 Thessalonians 3:5 ESV

See the Good in the Bad

The blistery cold nights of winter have frozen over our house and our hearts. My mom hasn't been herself for four months now. Today is January 31, 2020. It seems when things couldn't have gotten worse they did in terms of her health. Both physically and mentally, my mom is now a shell of a body. Her legs are so tiny they resemble two long hockey sticks with some padding on top. Her hands and wrists are the tiniest I've ever seen them, like two twigs from a red birch tree. When I visited her on Sunday, she said to me, "How did you get so big and I got so small?" It's an accurate and direct question. It stumped me. I didn't know what to say. She also said she isn't ready to die. She said she has to go back to where she started from. My mom is not ready to roll over and die just yet.

What could possibly be her mission now? What is on her heart that she would be fighting so fiercely at this point?

Waking up at 5 a.m. this morning came easy. My first thought was, "I feel better. My headache and tummy ache are gone ... but my energy feels slower." Today is the morning I feel older. Will I ever go back? Watching my mom go through this last stage of life is life sucking and just plain miserable. Everything strong and wonderful about my mother is still there, just minimized to the tiniest degree. Like she said, how did she get so small so fast? I could have said to her, "Well Mom you stopped eating in September.

You eat one meal a day, 25% of it at best." But I didn't. I held her hand and looked her in the eyes and I said, "Mom, what are you afraid of? You're God's girl and you've done a good job here on Earth and have nothing to fear." She immediately tilted her head back and clenched her eyes in a silent cry. She cried out with no tears left. Then as quickly as she cried, she looked back to me with a wild look and two tiny tears came down her face. That was all her body had left for hydration that day.

It would repeat several more times. Each time I told her how much I loved her, how I would be okay whenever she chose to leave this Earth, how she has done a job well done, and she would tilt her head back and would try to cackle like a rooster, yet all that would come out was a stifled long sigh. A sigh that held itself for four to five seconds then ended with a deep breath in and her eyes would widen and fixate on me again. And then the loving words came out. She said in a high-pitched squeal of a voice, "I thought you were going to flush me down the toilet! Vaginas! The dog Blue! The dog Blue!"

Whenever she is psychotic, I always try to find some hidden meaning in her words. I asked her if Blue was the dog that bit her when she was a young girl. She nodded yes. I asked her if Blue scared her and she nodded yes. I asked her if she was scared to die. She tilted her head back and mouth opened wide for another silent shriek of a cry. I can't say for certain if any of that is true. I don't know who the heck Blue was, although I do know my mom at the age five or six years old was deathly afraid of dogs after getting bitten by one on a winter afternoon while going ice skating with her family. Apparently, the dog bit into her buttocks and would not let go.

When school came back into session after Christmas break, the children were required to walk to St. Mary's School, which was only a block or two from her house. Yet a different dog lived next door, and my mom was paralyzed with fear to walk past it. At the time, her mother had other small children and babies at home, and I don't know how attentive she was to my mom. What I do know is her father found her not walking to school and gave her a swift punishment of a lashing on her bottom. So, my mom received her doom regardless. She never forgot that beating, and that was a foreshadowing of the future relationship with her father. No wonder my poor mother had the life she did. She never stood a chance from age six.

Knowing now what kind of loving, present, and candid person my mom is makes me cry on the inside for her, because I know she did not have that kind of mother. A mother that had the time to investigate and be aware would have realized why she didn't want to go to school. And a patient father like Michael Landon in *Little House on the Prairie* would have taken the time to get down on his knees and kindly ask my mother why she was afraid to walk to school. But no. No such father ever did that. It was a lashing that made her bleed. And it turned her little hands white with fear.

I just want to run up to that little girl and wrap my arms around her. I want to kiss her tears away and tell her it's all okay. One day it will all be okay. But was it ever okay? Would it be a lie? Would I have to tell her that things will only get harder? That her living situation will be covered over by the dark cloud of mental illness? That she would marry the love of her life only to go through divorce? That by age 60 she would be in a home? That by 75 her legs would be down to hockey sticks?

It's a bleak projection of a life, and I myself sit back in my chair and think, "My God. And she's still fighting for this? She won't turn away. Something is unsettled."

Like my mother told me at age eight when I asked her if God made the Earth then who made God, she turned to me and said, "Becky, some things are meant to be a mystery." I suppose this is one of those things. The older I get and the wiser I get, the more control I let go of, and I realize that I will never really understand it all. There is a sweet surrender in that. I don't have to figure it all out! I can rest in the Lord, I can rest in my creator. I can rest in the beauty of the world.

Even as I read over the last few sentences on this page and I'm covered in tears, I can see and feel the good. I can see my mother decorating the Christmas tree and putting baby Jesus underneath. I can hear Elvis Presley Christmas music in the background. I can feel her rocking me as a child in the creaky 1960s wooden square rocker chair with orange plaid upholstery. I can hear it's knocking in a rhythmic pattern. I can feel her soft arms around me and smell her perfume. I want to get her a rocking chair in her nursing home. I wonder if it's even possible and if I could rock my tiny child of a mother and calm her fears and tell her it's going to be okay. There's a better place just around the corner. A place with golden lit fields of sunflowers and a solar home with God at the heart of it. I want to rock her and wrap her up in my arms and just take away every pain that's in her creaky and unsettled bones. I want to see her get her real teeth back. Her running legs. Her speed and her mind. Her heart.

Chapter 4

THE ONES WE CARE FOR HAVE THE POWER TO BRING US DOWN

"All praise to God, the Father of our Lord Jesus Christ. God is our merciful Father and the source of all comfort. He comforts us in all our troubles so that we can comfort others. When they are troubled, we will be able to give them the same comfort God has given us. For the more we suffer for Christ, the more God will shower us with his comfort through Christ."

–2 Corinthians 1:3–5 NLT

Oftentimes I notice when my mom is down, I'm down. I can't explain this but when my mom is sick or physically ill, and there have been many UTIs and infections this last year, I will get something minor that mirrors her sickness. For example, last week Mom's whole mental state drastically changed. She became more withdrawn and delusional. She just wasn't herself. We know her pattern. She gets back to back UTIs. She is a DNR (do not resuscitate), so if she comes down with an infection, we do not treat her with antibiotics. Instead, we give her plenty of fluids and meds to keep her comfortable. Right now, she is on 15-minute checks. I know it must seem cruel that we have chosen this route. However, it's February of 2020 and she is 76 years old with a low quality of life. She is also physically strong and has fought off countless infections in the last two years. Too many to count. All without antibiotics.

My friend Christy likes to call her supernatural because she has these amazing swings from death back up to life again. She gets down to not eating, drinking, or breathing only to one day stand up out of bed and ask for a hot dog! (True story). My mom's timeline of life is none of my business. It's personal ... between her and the Lord.

Currently she is not in any pain. I'm sure it isn't comfortable, but she is asked often if she has pain. Her answer is always no. She is on Morphine. She is bedridden for the most part. She is mentally off. Yet she does not complain. Here I am in the early morning (6 a.m.) typing this up with a terrible cold. I feel like my head has been squeezed by a ruthless toddler refusing to loosen his grip. My body aches and my neck is cramped up. I've had a seven-day headache. I cough all night with nothing to come out. I feel miserable. But I'm not the one dying.

My Uncle John is an MD, and he educated me about End of Life cycles. He told me that when you reach End of Life you have many hospital visits. Back to back infections. This is a signal that you've entered the End of Life phase. Each time my mom comes out of an infection, she's a little less strong than she was before that sickness. She loses weight and can't get back more weight even with an appetite. My mom has been holding steady now at 97 lbs. The body is so strong! But the suffering while you are in your End of Life is tremendous. While I don't believe my mom is in any pain, I do think she is restless, uncomfortable, and even depressed over her life phase. Once, while she had a moment of clarity, I asked her if this life phase is harder than when she was a young mom with SZ, and she said, "Oh yes Honey, this phase is definitely harder." I know she's speaking the truth, because she's had to give up her independence, her freedom, her mind, and her body. It's a total surrender of heart and soul.

I often contemplate why she's still here and what she needs to work out with the Lord. I've prayed to her and read the Bible to her, but so far, she has had a very quiet faith. While I respect that, I often wonder if she knew the God I knew … if she knew about the truth of total acceptance of Jesus, that by simply asking Him to enter your heart, you will be saved. I wonder if she knew it was that simple and she didn't need to follow rules and be a certain way or act a certain way. God loves us just the way we are! Truly I know she had taught me this as a child. But her mental state prevents her from believing it for herself. I want my mom to feel Christ's love in fullness, to receive the Holy Spirit, to be in awe of the miracle of just believing. If I could wish for one thing before she passes, it's for her to feel the complete joy of being a child of God.

So I say this simple prayer:

Dear Lord,

On behalf of my dear mother, I ask that You would be with her now. Fill her with Your Holy Spirit. Remind her of the beautiful gifts she has. Give her comfort, Lord, in these times of suffering. Quench her thirst when she's thirsty. Give comfort when she's afraid. Offer her joy, Lord, during her last days on Earth. Give me the strength as her daughter to help aid in this beautiful transition back to You and Your kingdom.

Amen.

The Maze

In December 2018, I reached a low point in all of my caregiving history. It began with the lie that my mom was never going to find a nursing home to live in. She had been admitted into three different hospitals in a few months span, and she was declining both mentally and physically. Only 75 years old at the time, which society thinks is old, I was not ready to give up on my mom. I was determined to find a long-term placement for her that would fit all of her needs. She had an exhausting list. She needed a nursing home that also had a memory care unit, would help her with bathing, meds, and feeding, and would take her to her appointments. She had broken her foot and required a brace, yet she fought the brace and wanted nothing to do with it. It caused her great irritation. She needed monthly blood draws. She had developed upper GI bleeding that required monitoring. She needed monthly well visits for her mental health, and she needed on-call psychiatric care to monitor her lithium levels and Clozaril levels. I also needed her to be close to me so I could visit her often. The connection that I had with my mom needed to be maintained. The list of requirements seemed so long and seemed impossible to acquire. I was beginning to lose hope.

The local nursing home in town told me they would never admit a resident with mental illness. They said no nursing home around here would do that. I was horrified. I called anyone who was willing to listen to me and help me find a permanent home for my mom. I called Aging and Disability Resource Center, I called the county and human services. I called my friend Sarah who owned homes for the disabled; I asked anyone I knew that might have an idea. I tried getting her on a list at a nursing home in town across the street from the YMCA because I knew my mom's love of swimming (at least when she was younger). I was picturing her getting better and being able to do these things. I didn't realize or want to realize the decline that was coming our way. That nursing home after weeks of conversation and negotiation decided my mom was too much a risk to take in.

I was walking through my living room and I had just gotten off the phone with another nursing home that told me no. It was a major blow. They said they would consider my mom in the future, but not now. If she lived somewhere else successfully for two months, she could maybe transfer in. I didn't want her to have to move again and again. I wanted to get her into a long-term option, one that would take care of her to every level of need that she deserved.

As my mind raced, I pictured my mother living forever in the hospital with no permanent address. I felt my heart flutter and my palms sweat. I was entering Panic Zone. Out of desperation, I walked straight to the front door and swung it wide open. It was snowy outside and I felt the cold wind rush over my body and bring me back to earth. I had just had a full-blown panic attack. I was filled with fear for the future.

UNBINDING *Love*

Looking back, I wish I could have known that help was right around the corner, that sometimes we have to have the freak out before we have the freedom. God has it under control, but we don't realize it because we're too caught up in our own junk. We can only see what's right in front of our faces. But our Loving God is so powerful. He is not limited like how we are limited.

My mom was eventually transferred to another hospital, then at that hospital the social worker asked me about Lakeview Health Center, located eight miles from my house. Not only did they have a unit with staff especially trained for dementia, it was a behavioral health unit so she would have a psych doctor in house. It was a huge win for us. They came to the hospital and met her and instantly liked her (She was having a good day and was all smiles thankfully!). They opened up a room for her in their 10-bed unit, and she has been there ever since.

THE ONES WE CARE FOR HAVE THE POWER TO BRING US DOWN

They have been the perfect fit for my mom. When I think about Lakeview Health Center and all the love and precise care they've given my mom, I get instantly emotional. God knew Lainey had a home. He knew she would be safe. I was the only one filled with doubt. Looking back, I wish I could have reassured myself at the time that everything would be okay. It's hard when we are stuck in the maze of life and can't see what direction we're going. We have to be constantly reassured that God knows exactly what's happening, and furthermore that He wants us to get through it.

"From the end of the earth I call to you, when my heart is faint. Lead me to the rock that is higher than I." –Psalm 61:2

God wants us to know He's got it under control. He can see us and where we are going, but to us, it feels like we're stuck in a maze, like we are never going to get out. I'm telling you, He is in control. He knows what will happen; He wants you to come to Him so He can give you a play by play of where to go.

Dear Father,

Please help me to see which direction to go. I'm tired and weary, and I don't know what the solution is to my problem. Help make that solution clear to me today, Lord. Help me to see how to get out of the maze. You said in the Bible that when I call on You, You will lead me to a higher rock. Help me get to that rock Lord. Thank You for Your blessings, Your vision, and Your faithfulness Lord God. You never let me down.

In Your Name I pray!

Are you feeling you've lost hope for your future? Are you feeling like God has forgotten you? Get out your notebook and spend 10 minutes writing down all your fears and anxieties. Lay them before the Lord. Then pray over them and ask for help. Ask the Lord to grant you the Holy Spirit to address each and every need. Today. Ask Him for the living waters to be washed over you. He is waiting for you to come to Him.

The devil wants us to fear the future. He will access us in any way possible. Through fights with our spouse, tiredness, even sometimes he gets to us while we sleep at night. Just last night I had a dream. I was giving a speech in front of a lot of people and I was doing a terrible job! Then after that dream, I dreamed I was mentally so sick I had to see a doctor myself for psych meds. I woke up with a pounding headache and achy body. Satan didn't want me to get to writing this book. So, I made a cup of coffee and slowly moved my body. When I put my body in motion, the first thing I did was grab my armor, my Bible. I sat down, and I realized I couldn't find my morning devotional, my daily guidance to my Bible. After searching for over an hour, I found it hidden underneath a pillow on my chair. I read today's Bible message and it was the message I wrote above in Psalm 61. Thank You, Lord, for showing me that You are in control and You will take care of me when I am tired and lost. Every morning when I seek Him, He shows me His tenderness and compassion by giving me the right word at the right time. I can't make this up! The Holy Spirit will come to you in the most surprising ways! The spirit will bring you peace when you are overcome with fear. Try it.

Don't be afraid to allow God to move mountains in your life. You have nothing to lose.

Anxiety

There's something I have to write and talk about that is very difficult for me to share. It involves exposing something about myself, a vulnerability, a disclaimer that I wouldn't feel right if I didn't share but that is tough to type nonetheless. I have a continuous fear that overplays in my mind. It's the question of, "Am I next?" And what I mean by that is am I going crazy? I've struggled with anxiety my whole life, especially postpartum anxiety. It was crippling at night, and it would leave me paralyzed until morning came. I still experience anxiety today, and I've realized some triggers such as certain foods and alcohol consumption and lack of sleep. But the anxiety always comes back, and when it does, it's always an unwelcomed guest, rocking me to the core.

After my oldest daughter Susan was born, to say I was exhausted would be an understatement. I literally was driving around town in my van and not knowing what the heck was going on. Like driving around in a cloud, I was so dazed I couldn't remember how to get to Festival Foods from my house. When I went for my eight-week postpartum check-up, my doctor asked me if I was taking iron. Nope. So, as it turns out, I was extremely anemic from giving birth via C-section, and I was operating on fumes.

Even after starting iron, it took me weeks then months to feel like a normal person again. I was still bleeding, my incision hurt, my baby was colic, and I hadn't slept in a year. I needed some vacation therapy. And that did not happen for me because I feared leaving my house. I remember the only time I would leave my house was to go to the grocery store. That was vital, I had to have food. (I was raised by a single mom on food stamps, trust me, food was and always will be a top priority in my life.) I remember clutching the steering wheel of my minivan, palms sweaty, and feeling my heart race. I wasn't really worried about anything except for the fact of what if I couldn't drive this vehicle home? Who will take care of my baby? What if I collapse inside the grocery store and someone has to resuscitate me? What would others think of me if they knew I had this anxiety? They would think I'm crazy.

I've literally been so anxious at times I pull out my cell phone just to look at calming pictures or distract my brain from panic. This is no way to live. I created a reality where my brain could create fear at any second of the day. And this fear started to cripple me. As my baby grew older and started sleeping better, I started to come back to life and get some sleep, and the anxiety quieted. It has never fully gone away, but it is a small cry once in a while versus a habitual clashing thunderstorm.

How can the fear of anxiety hold so much dang power over me, when in reality most of the time I don't have it? I'm free and healthy and happy, and I realize that when I go see my doctor, everything checks out on the blood panel. Yup, I'm 100% healthy again. Oh, darn it. Because Doc I feel like I'm going to die. Or maybe it's the fear I'm going to die? Or maybe it's the fear that I fear about dying? I can't keep it straight. Gosh darn it, I'm a fearful person. I just tend to be a worrier, and at night especially, I will conjure up all sorts of awful scenarios. I swear our brains don't function the same at night, and when my brain stops working, I wonder if that's how my mom's brain is all the time. Is her brain always overtired and overthinking and worrying? I don't know. I don't know what it feels like to be

THE ONES WE CARE FOR HAVE THE POWER TO BRING US DOWN

her, but I know what it feels like to be crippled with anxiety. The worst is when a wave of panic comes over my body for no absolute reason and I think to myself, "Okay, is this it? Is this when they're going to put me into an ambulance and lock ME up?"

The reason why I'm sharing this with you, beloved reader, is because I'm guessing you may have faced this same fear. Even if you've never experienced a moment of anxiety in your life, you have experienced fear. It comes in many different shapes and sizes. It does not discriminate and it does not care how educated, funny, sensible, and likeable you are. Like one of my favorite song lyrics says:

Fear, he is a liar
He will take your breath
Stop you in your steps

Fear fear he is a liar
He will rob your rest
Steal your happiness

Cast your fear in the fire
Cause fear he is a liar.[2]

So take that fear, whatever it looks like to you, and cast it in the fire. How I do that is I say out loud, "Satan, I know you're trying to fill me with anxiety right now so I don't finish my book. Satan, I'm going to finish the book. And when you wake me up at night to fill fear in me, I'm going to pray for all my neighbors down the street and all the

---

[2] Williams, Z. (2016). Fear is a Liar [Song]. On *Chain Breaker*. Essential.

missionaries in my church. I'm going to do triple time for the good side Lord if you wake me up one more time, I swear." Saying it out loud that FEAR and ANXIETY hold no control is very empowering. Yell it out. Say it out. Speak it out. Whisper it out. It is so good to declare today that none of those things shall hold power over you because none of those things are of God. Only God is capable of perfect love.

Dear Lord,

Thank You, Lord Jesus, for loving me in the perfect way. I know even when You came to Earth as human, You must have felt incredible fear. I can't imagine the fear You felt on the cross, the day they beat You and tried to humiliate You. They failed, and today You are the Lion, the king, the redeemer. Lord, please take that fire You have and heal me and my heart from any fear or anxiety. Lord, just take any moment of doubt I have, any disturbing thoughts about myself or my health or my life, Lord, and just throw them into the fire. Fill me with Your love, Your faith, Your trust. Help me to see my worth through Your eyes Lord Jesus. I can only find true love like that from You, my Savior.

Thank You, Lord, in Your Name I pray!

Don't Worry—Be Adventurous

You don't have to climb Mt. Everest or backpack across Europe to find adventure. Have you ever heard that adventure awaits in your own backyard? Why do so many people think they have to do outrageous things like eat a bucket of beetles and cross the Amazon in a canoe to wear the badge of courage? I would argue that adventure is knocking on our door every day, but many of us are too consumed, too tired, and too worried to hear the knock.

Worry is my middle name. Growing up, it seemed I was afraid of everything. When I was little, I worried about thunderstorms. I also had recurring dreams that robbers were entering our home and my mom was too weak to fend them off. I'd get so scared in my dreams that my ears would ring until a screaming alarm would fill my head. I'd wake up in panic mode. I guess I had anxiety even as a small girl. After the dreams, I would carry out my day waiting for the sky to fall.

As I grew older and started high school, around the end of my freshman year, my mom had a year or so of mental stability. She laughed a lot, enjoyed shopping with her friends, and loved making me homemade French toast with strawberries and Philadelphia whipped cream on top. I was only visiting her on the weekends, but our time was so precious to me. I needed her that summer because life was accelerating for me. I had my first boyfriend, was curious about the world, and was looking for that role model to fill me up with wisdom.

One night, as the muggy air filled my mom's apartment (again, she didn't believe in air conditioning), she said in an excited voice, "Let's go to the bars!" I thought I heard her wrong. "What!?" But I couldn't help but feel excited. There was a boy in my creative drama class who bartended on the weekends because he was 18. His name was Don, and he was the star of the class, always excited to be there and putting on a show with his overzealous acting. Let's be clear here, he had big muscles. I quickly agreed, and Mom and I got ready for the bars. I put on a nice pink blouse with ruffles and matching pink lipstick, and mom combed her hair and added on those angry looking black brows like she always did.

I don't remember if we walked or drove, but the bar that I suggested where Don worked was only a few blocks from my mom's apartment on Johnson Street in Oshkosh. We walked in and sat down at the bar, and mom ordered me a soda. Clearly, we didn't go for the drinking! Still to this day, I don't know why my mom wanted to go to the bars. Maybe she was feeling good about herself. I'd like to picture that and her realizing that she was still beautiful, still had it together, and could turn a few heads and order a soda in a smoky, dingy small bar.

Going to the bar was hardly like climbing a mountain, but it was exhilarating to feel grown up and feel like a woman myself with my mom, safely exploring the boundaries of the world with her next to me. The boy wasn't working that night, and I was left with a "That's all there is to it?" thinking, but in the end, my mom made a bold move with me that felt a little risky and adventurous, when in fact she stayed completely in control. Later down the road we even laughed about our wild night out to the bars.

Is there something you've been wanting to do, create, or learn? Have you been wanting to try a hobby or learn a new language? Investing in yourself as a caregiver will benefit you greatly. Being adventurous is the positive way of saying, "Don't worry." You know what happens to me when people tell me, "Don't worry"? That's right—I worry. So instead of me telling you not to worry, I am urging you to find adventure in your day, today. If you are a person who thrives on routine, wake up tomorrow and switch up your day. Instead of brushing your teeth, throw on a bathrobe and go outside and watch the birds. Or watch the sun rise. Or I don't know, do something crazy you never do like watch old reruns of Jeopardy and eat ice cream in your living room.

Adventure looks different to different people. Allow yourself the freedom to be creative and to check in with yourself and see what you need. I know I need more adventure in my life when things start to feel like I'm on repeat each day. The days look the same and I laugh a little less and the worry lines pop out of my forehead. Trust me, I am the guiltiest of this! Ha! I worry about being a worrier. How funny is that?

Dare Yourself To:

Go for a walk in the rain.

Eat breakfast for supper and supper for breakfast.

Stay up late one night just to binge on your favorite TV show.

Wake up early, go on a nature walk, and sit in nature and see what God is telling you to do next.

Call up an old childhood friend. Tell them you still think about them.

Write a book about your life.

Quit the job you don't love and start doing what you love.

If you're single, sign up for online dating.

If you're married, plan a fun date your spouse doesn't know about.

Sleep in the guest bedroom of your home. It's vacation at home! Make the bed beautiful and put a water next to the bed and relax.

If you have children, get a babysitter one day and just sit in the quiet house and allow yourself to dream and think.

If you have a disabled adult child at home, ask a friend or family member to take them out for the day so you can boldly do something for you.

Sign up to run a 5K, 10K, or half marathon. Then every morning run for a few minutes and build up endurance. Sometimes running isn't about the exercise, it's about doing something for you and showing others you can do it.

Learn a new foreign language.

Make a new random friend that you meet at Walmart. Tell them you're looking for a friend and that you will pray for them. Extra credit: Friend someone who isn't your age.

These ideas may seem silly or even stupid, but I guarantee you they will add a little fizz back into your cup. We all need to be rejuvenated in some way, and our bodies and our minds crave activity, movement, and exploration. Think of how you were as a child. You were always up for adventure! Your body pulsed with activity, you loved to learn about life, and you were constantly up for a playdate with others. We need to decide to channel that energy back into our beings. We can do this! We can be fun, it just takes a small step of intention.

Your exercise for the end of the chapter is to get out your notebook and write down all the crazy things you want to do with your life. I dare you to go bold, but they can be small too. No one else will read it, so have fun with it! After you've made your list, circle your top three and then go out and do that. Make a step towards those goals today. You can be adventurous and still a caregiver. God made you to be creative; he made you smart and capable. He wants you to boldly declare that your life matters and your dreams matter and that from now on you will not let these dreams slip by.

I declare on _____ (today's date) that _____ (my name) will live a life of bold, adventurous caregiving. I will no longer ignore my dreams, hopes, and goals. I will do small things today that bring me to living a fun life, one that I'm proud of.

Thank You, Lord, for giving me my creativity to try new things.

Laughing Is the Best Medicine

All throughout my childhood, my mom had several make-believe boyfriends. They usually switched about every five to eight years. I think they changed names with each move that took place. The longest relationship she has ever had is her current relationship with country western singer Toby Keith. They've been together since the early 2000s. She bought many of his albums and often plays his music in her CD player at the nursing home. All the nurses that tend to my mom know she's in love with the country western star. They ask her how Toby is and my mom will have a huge grin on her face and blush and really feel all the nervous feelings of being in love with a man. She usually replies, "Toby Keith! He's special! Do you think I'm pretty enough to marry him? Maybe I'll have some plastic surgery ..."

Before Toby it was "The Egg Man and the Indian." Yes, this is one man. I have never figured out who this mysterious man was, but she was obsessed with him and would often say, "I think I'll marry him ... if he still wants me." Most of her boyfriends were protective, loving, and didn't want her showing any cleavage. That's what she told me. Apparently, these men were all "brawny," she said, and very "manly." She also has made some sexual comments to me over the years about them that have made me very uncomfortable.

For example, the time she lived in Red Granite at Pine Hills Assisted Living she had a week of poor sleep. We were all concerned maybe a psychotic relapse was coming. To help her before it got worse, she voluntarily admitted herself to the ER to get a sleeping aid. While waiting in a tiny hospital room, I noticed it was divided into two rooms with a shower curtain. Apparently, this hospital was overcrowded and they had to divide up some of the rooms. There was a man next door who sounded like he was in some major pain. A lot of pain. You could hear him moaning and groaning in agony.

All of a sudden out of nowhere, as my mother laid on the stretcher, she yelled really loudly, "I HAD A THIRTY MINUTE ORGASM! I KNOW YOU DON'T BELIEVE ME BECKY. BUT I DID. I MEAN IT WAS SO GLORIOUS. A THIRTY MINUTE ORGASM!" And her speech was a little slurred like she had had too much to drink at the bar (even though she hadn't), and she continued to repeat this over and over. I would try to settle her down. There was a guy dying next door and somehow, I couldn't let this be the last thing he heard. Oh gosh, but it was so funny. I recorded it and still have it on my iPhone to this day.

Besides the fact my mother has continually embarrassed me, she has given me a good laugh or two. This is so necessary in life. I feel sorry for those who are so uptight they forget to laugh. I know how it feels to be plagued with worry, I'm one of those people. To lay awake at night thinking, "What will happen to Mom? How will her end days be? What will it be like once she's gone to Heaven?" I don't know the answers to those questions, and that causes me great anxiety sometimes.

The unknown is like a wide-open dark sea with hidden creatures inside just waiting to bite at my legs. Or it could be a rushing calm sea that hugs me like a cooling blanket. Or a combination of both. Who knows? One thing I know for sure is you need to allow yourself to have humor and use it to your advantage. Laughing at the small stuff is so useful (and who knows, maybe even the big stuff!). Humor gives us permission to laugh. To let go. To just be in the moment. If you don't have a comedian in your life like I had my mother, just watch a really funny movie once in a while. Studies have shown there's healing in laughter. Life can't be so serious all the time.

Questions:

1. When was the last time you laughed belly roll laughs?

2. What are your fears? Have you ever experienced crippling anxiety? (Read the Bible passages on anxiety if you have!)

3. What does God say about fear in the Bible?

Chapter 5

WHAT YOU CAN DO TO MAKE A DIFFERENCE

"Rejoice in hope, be patient in tribulation, be constant in prayer."

–Romans 12:12 ESV

How to Talk to Someone With Schizophrenia

"In the day that I'm afraid, I lay all my fears before you and trust in you with all my heart. What harm could a man bring to me? With God on my side I will not be afraid of what comes. The roaring praises of God fill my heart, and I will always triumph as I trust his promises." –Psalm 56:3–4 TPT

A common frustration among caregivers is the fact that communication is very little or near impossible with their loved one. To demonstrate this fact, I will explain a conversation that took place with my mom a few months ago. It was January 23, 2020 and my mom had just recovered from another near-death experience. As she has gotten older, her cycles are coming faster and more severe. So, for two weeks she'll be fine and then two weeks she'll stop eating, drinking, and walking. It's the strangest thing. Like a radio station coming in and out of tuning, so does her brain. It is difficult to keep track, and you're never quite prepared for anything.

My mother had just recovered from plummeting down to 88 pounds for no reason and was put on Morphine to pass away. She had stopped most bodily functions and the nurses told me she should pass by Christmas. Guess what? She didn't. She rallied. She came back and she had the best day ever since her near-death experience. I showed up to the nursing home to check up on her, not expecting any sort of conversation to take place. Actually, at that time she was sleeping mostly during the day so it was tough to catch her awake. When I stepped in, not only was she awake and smiling, but she asked me to crawl into bed with her and snuggle. That's right. My mother who was crying out a week ago for a "bucket of blood" was now asking me to climb in and spoon. So of course, I took off my shoes and thoroughly enjoyed snuggling with my mama, something I hadn't done in over 30 years.

As soon as she opened her mouth, I knew she was in the mood to talk and it was going to be entertaining. So, I grabbed my iPhone and started recording on the memo app. I figured if she did kick the can soon, it would be nice to have her voice documented.

Mom: Sometimes I have little aches and pains, but I will *never* go back to your father again. Did you know he has his tombstone there? (My dad is still living btw.)

Me: No, I didn't know that ...

Mom: Yup. In Oshkosh. Not the country singer. Who do I like? That's special? With the furniture?

WHAT YOU CAN DO TO MAKE A DIFFERENCE

Me: You have furniture together?

Mom: Yeah.

Me: Toby Keith?

Mom: Yeah, Toby Keith ... Not the country singer.

Me: Well, who are you talking about then?

Mom: (laughs)

Me: (laughs) Who are you talking about?

Mom: Maybe I'm rotten at sex.

Me: What??

Mom: Maybe I'm (muffled) at sex.

Me: I don't even understand what you're saying.

Mom: Okay, we won't talk about it.

Me: I'm glad you wanted to snuggle with me, it's been a while.

Mom: It has been a while. It's the good ol' days.

Me: We're spooning.

Mom: Are we spooning like you and Norm? (Norm apparently is the new name for my husband. His real name is Matthew.)

Me: (laughs) Well his name is Matthew.

Mom: (laughs) Matthew is his first name?

Me: Yes, you call him Stewart.

Mom: Who's Stewart? Last name.

UNBINDING *Love*

Me: That's right, that's his last name. You call him by his last name.

Mom: And it's Norm.

Me: (laughs) You keep calling him Norm.

Mom: What's his first name?

Me: Matthew.

Mom: Matthew Stewart.

Me: Yup.

Mom: And it was wild last night when you came with the four kids.

Me: Was it wild?

Mom: It was wild! We had to put you in a special bed.

Me: I didn't come with the kids yesterday.

Mom: That was yesterday?

Me: *You* said it was yesterday.

Mom: You said it was Sunday! (laughs)

Me: (laughs) OK. The kids weren't here on Sunday either. It was just me.

Mom: Just you?

Me: Yeah.

Mom: The one I like?

Me: That's me!

Mom: You drove here?

WHAT YOU CAN DO TO MAKE A DIFFERENCE

Me: Yes.

Mom: I thought you came with the kids?

Me: Nope.

Mom: You were wild! (laughs)

Me: (laughs)

Mom: And who did I say I'm in love with?

Me: Toby Keith!

Mom: Toby Keith the country singer?

Me: Yeah!

Mom: I'm in love with Toby Keith the country singer?

Me: Yeah, that's what you told me.

Mom: What's his first name?

Me: Toby.

Mom: Toby Keith?

Me: Yeah.

Mom: You see, you called me up and told me you were worried about the solar power and we had a tornado and I called somebody up and I said um you called me up and you were upset, and she said the solar power was crackly and there were drugs under the solar power.

Me: (Laughs) There were *drugs* under the solar power?

Mom: Yeah, not the solar power, just drugs, and you were under your house, and you came into the basement.

Me: Why did I come into the basement?

Mom: Because it was an emergency. And I don't want the country singer. I want the one that ... who was the country singer?

Me: Toby Keith.

Mom: I don't want him. I want a different one I thought.

Me: Okay.

Mom: David!

Me: You want David?

Mom: Yup, David.

Then she starts singing a song she made up about popsicles. There's more to this conversation but you get the point.

Meet Them Where They Are At

In the above situation, my mom was feeling happy and ready to talk. She talked and talked and some of it made sense and some of it did not. That's okay. When she says stuff that is crazy and I know it's not the truth, I say, "Okay." I don't remind her she's not right. I don't crush her dreams. One of her biggest goals in life is to marry Toby Keith. I am not going to be the one to tell her that isn't possible. Instead, I listen and reaffirm her. It doesn't hurt her to believe in the goodness of having a love in her life. Now, when she says Toby is going to start taking her to her appointments, then I still might agree but also remind her that she has a care team that does that and maybe she shouldn't be so dependent on a man. That helps her. Her eyes widen and she says, "Okay," and laughs. So, you meet them where they're at.

If they are sad, you get quiet and say, "I'm so sorry you feel sad. I'm here for you." Many days my mom does not want to talk much at all. That's okay because I'm meeting her where she's at and I'm not forcing her into something she's not ready or able to carry out. Many times, my mom is not capable of being a mother to me. Just like many times your son/daughter, your spouse, will not be capable of being that role to you. It is unfair for us to put that kind of pressure onto them because their brains simply are on overload and they are only capable of so much.

That's not to say you will be happy with that arrangement. That's not to say you won't feel sad when you're having a bad day and you want to connect with your loved one. I can remember clearly a moment in my life where I needed my mom. I needed my mom to be a mom to me. It was the Friday before Mother's Day and my second oldest daughter was four at the time and in preschool. That morning, all the kids put on a special Mother's Day breakfast at their preschool and instead of remembering to go, I was home nursing my newborn and dozing off on a nap. The phone rang and startled me. I had been startled thinking I must have slept through pick up. But the teacher reminded me about the Mother's Day breakfast and how much Lucy was looking forward to me being there. I felt so embarrassed, and even worse, hurt that I let my daughter down.

As I approached the preschool, I saw Lucy standing outside with her teachers with her hand on her hip. "You forgot again, Mom," she said matter-of-factly. I felt about as small as a twig on the branch of the tree next to us. As I drove home from the preschool with my two littles in the back of the van, tears welled in my eyes and my heart began to race. I grabbed my phone and dialed the number at my mom's assisted living. When they got her on the phone with me, I cried and let everything out like an animal that was dying and needed resuscitation. She listened very carefully, and then in a calm and sweet voice she said, "Oh Becky, that isn't so bad. There are so many worse things in the world. So what if you missed the breakfast?" It calmed me down and helped me to breathe and even more so, it taught me that my mother *could* still be a mom to me. That she could still have my back. That she loved me still no matter how many times I messed up.

After that conversation, and after I got both girls down for a nap, I called my mom back again. I wanted more. I wanted to connect with her again and thank her for the love and advice she gave me.

Me: Mom, I just want to thank you for all the wonderful advice you gave me. It really means a lot.

Mom: Sure honey.

Me: Um, hey do you think we could talk some more? Like about life and all the things we've missed talking about the past few years?

Mom: Well, the women in our family always did have tight vaginas.

And that was the end of our connection!

I realized that God gave me a window. He gave me what I needed at the time. I was not granted a mother that was cured from Schizophrenia. I was given a small glimpse, a small gift that was to be treasured. I smiled and told my mom we could talk another day. And deep down, the little bit of connection we had really meant so much more to me than I think it would have otherwise.

Expect Less, Hope for More

In terms of conversation, never expect your loved one to be ready to talk to you. In fact, when you picture connecting with them, know that if it happens it is rare and it is a blessing. When you need facts from them, they may not be able to tell you. You might have to investigate and provide help based on not what they say but by what they do. It's okay. There is no perfection in your caretaking, so there is no perfection in your communication either.

Once you let go of the concept of how you "should" be communicating, it gives you freedom to allow the communication to happen on their terms. It is much easier said than done. You will find it frustrating in the beginning. You will have days where you explode and demand they answer your question. This is not operating out of a place of rest and a place of love. Anytime you are demanding in your caregiving you need to take a step back. You need to ask yourself if you're following self-care, taking care of yourself, and establishing good boundaries—are you safe and are they safe? Once all those boxes are checked, you will be in a rested place where you will not put so much pressure on your loved one to operate the way you wish they would. You won't put any expectations on them.

Along with letting go of the high expectations in your communication, always look for opportunities to connect with them. Maybe there will be an awkward moment where they aren't making any sense and they realize it and you have a good laugh. Laugh with them. That is a moment that you can capture. I am always taking pictures with my mom. We do selfies and sometimes her hair is standing straight up and later we laugh about it. She usually says she's ugly, and then I tell her, "No you're beautiful." It's a funny exchange. I am so happy I have pictures with my mom. They are imperfect and they are weird and they are funny, and yet they ARE MINE. She is mine. It looks nothing like the relationship my best friend has with her mom. And that's okay. Our relationship is what it is. It is raw, beautiful, funny, sad, devastating, and rewarding all in one.

Only God is capable of relationships like that! Only He can make something so beautiful out of something so hard. So never lose hope in having a connection here or there. It usually comes out of the blue when I'm not expecting it. Sometimes I will even dread visiting my mom. I never quite know what mood she'll be in and I don't want to be hurt. Some days I'm tired. But it's like pulling off a Band-Aid. You go and do it because it's the right thing to do. And you never regret going. I give myself permission to visit her on shortened visits that last maybe 10 minutes when she is mentally off. Some days I just can't handle it. And that's okay. It's knowing what I'm capable of that day and knowing what I can do in my caregiving. Some days I need a mental health day. Some days I need to check out.

WHAT YOU CAN DO TO MAKE A DIFFERENCE

Ignore Threats and Put Downs

About a year ago, my mom was hospitalized for a UTI that moved into a pretty serious blood infection. She was put on very heavy antibiotics and her body did fight it, but it was looking grim at the time. Whenever her body is working hard physically to fight something, her mental health goes right down the tubes. As you can guess, she was highly psychotic even though just days before she was perfectly calm and at her baseline.

I had come to visit her at the hospital and as soon as I walked in, my mom glared me down like I was the bad guy. Her eyes looked red and she had a snarl on her lips, and I knew she was out for blood. The first thing she said to me was she asked me why I was wearing those ugly earrings.

They were gold dangle earrings in the shape of hearts, and I thought they were pretty cute.

Me: You don't like my earrings?

Mom: And that *ugly* coat. That is such an ugly coat.

Me: Yeah, it's pretty dirty from the winter. Maybe I should wash it?

Mom: NO. Throw that UGLY coat away. It's terrible. Why would you wear such an ugly coat? I HATE you!

And when she yelled "HATE" I swear the windows in the hospital shook with vengeance.

Now, I could have taken it personally and told her back she looked like hell and she shouldn't talk like that. But I didn't. I smiled and said, "Mom you have such great fashion advice. I really should listen to you more." She just glared at me. In truth, nothing I'm going to say is really going to matter. She was mentally not well, so the reality was in a few days she wouldn't remember the conversation anyway. So, I took a deep breath and took the punches. I knew deep down she felt crummy and that's why she was lashing out at me. So, whenever that happens in your situation, let the threats go and remember it's the illness and not them. They really can't help it. They love you, but they have a disease. It's hard sometimes to separate them from the disease. But you must. It takes practice and patience.

Focus on Non-Verbal Communication When Verbal Isn't Possible

One of my favorite ways to talk to my mom actually doesn't involve talking at all. Some days when I go to visit her, if she's sleeping or resting, I just sit down next to her. I say a prayer over her and I revel in that I'm next to her in the same space just loving on her. The silence is nice and I don't have to listen to the chatter of ranting and rhyming. I can see her and the beauty of her face. When she opens her eyes, I'll say, "Good morning sunshine." If she's not happy to see me, sometimes I will do an experiment and just put my hand on top of hers. Or I will rub her shoulders and pat her down like a mother does to her baby toddler. She loves this. She will stare into my eyes and mostly say nothing. I realize that my mom is physically deprived of touch. All humans need it to thrive and survive. So, I try to offer her touch as often as I can. Some days I've done it and instead of accepting it, she will dig her nails into the soft flesh of my hands. That means back away and I usually end the visit there. I usually leave her be in her room. It is not a good day.

Examples of Non-Verbal Communication

Hugs

Kisses

Holding hands

Prayer

Helping them with a chore

Bringing them a cup of water or a snack (my mom loves potato chips)

Offering to put on their radio for them or playing music for them

Massage (my mom loves oils massaged on her feet)

Remember to meet them where they are at. If they are sad, don't walk in and smile ear to ear. Instead, offer them a soothing hug like you would to someone at a funeral. If they are happy and energetic and on a high, smile wide and pat them on the shoulders.

Sometimes if they are feeling sorry for themselves you can use humor to perk them up. I've done this with my mom and it usually is successful.

Mom: Oh Becky, you've got to get me out of this place. I'm going to go crazy in here.

Me: Okay Mom. I hear you. Well, we could use some help at our house with the kids. How about you come and live with us and be our nanny?

Mom: Nanny! Oh goodness no. (Laughs)

Me: Okay, well if it ever gets really bad just let me know. I also could use some help with the cooking and the laundry.

Mom stops laughing. She now thinks I'm serious.

I actually have used this over and over again and it works. She knows she does not want to help me raise my kids so she instead realizes it isn't so bad to live independently where she's at.

WHAT YOU CAN DO TO MAKE A DIFFERENCE

Having the Tough Talk About Suicide

My mom was 40 years old when her ex-boyfriend committed suicide. He was the first man she dated after the divorce with my father. They were not very serious, in fact I have no idea how they met. The only evidence of Jake was found in a Sweetest Day card he sent to my mom. He thanked her for being supportive and offered her a dinner date anytime she wanted. Inside the card, my mom taped a newspaper clipping of his obituary. In the obit, it was determined he died of suicide via carbon monoxide poisoning in his car. He was 30 years old.

Before that, my mom had a friend she met in a support group who also committed suicide. I have very few memories of her. I remember she smoked cigarettes and met my mom at Hardees in the late mornings for a breakfast platter. She was always kind to me but even as a kid I knew she had issues. She used to bob her legs up and down and she always seemed nervous. I think my mom was the mentoring one in the relationship and would try to help her out. I don't know any more details of her life or death. I don't know if she had children or a husband she left behind. I don't know her dreams or her fears or what she held close to her heart. I wonder what lies Satan told her to throw in the towel. I wonder if she had someone close to her to tell her she mattered, God had a purpose for her and her life, and no matter how down she got, she was *never* alone. I sadly will never know any of the answers to these questions.

The third and first exposure my mom had to suicide was the neighbor girl who grew up in a wonderful family and later married a wonderful husband. After delivering her baby, the postpartum depression was so bad she was sent to the mental ward at the hospital where she later died of a fire she set herself inside her hospital room. She set the room on fire with a cigarette. This haunted my mom and my mom's family for years. My grandma especially felt personal anguish over the loss of this young mother. At that time, in the 60s, mental illness had a stigma we can't relate to today. Yes, it still has stigma, but not like it held back then. Back then no one admitted to having a mental illness or asked anyone for help. I wonder what would have happened to this woman had she been born a few decades later when there would be NAMI (National Alliance on Mental Illness), friends, and family to support her with her postpartum depression.

Have the Conversation. Talk With Your Loved One About Suicide

Please have the tough conversation with them and ask them if they think about suicide. Try not to push the talk or make any expectations out of the talk, but please bring it up when your loved one is able to talk and seems to be wanting connection with you. Ask if they've ever attempted or came up with a plan. If the answer is no, great, you can stop the conversion. But if the answer is yes, please move forward with caution and compassion. Don't be afraid to go there and ask the hard follow-up questions. You can pivot into questions such as, "Tell me about a time when you felt like giving up. Tell me if you struggle with thoughts of suicide." Then after they've told you, rest your hand on their hand and tell them they matter to you. Tell them you are so glad you're close enough that you can confide in each other. Tell them you need them and you will do everything you can to help them so they don't ever go to despair.

Tell Them They Are Loved

This is so simple and seems ridiculous to type out, but please remind your loved one regularly that they are loved. Even when they are behaving badly, or saying mean things to you, or just don't believe they are deserving of love. Tell them. Tell them God the Father loves them very much and with time and prayer they will find healing and help. No, life is not perfect, but through hope in the Savior and hope for a better day tomorrow, day by day your loved one can find and feel improvement with their current situation.

Having a Faith in Christ Does Not Mean You Are Safe From Suicide

Just because your loved one has faith in Christ does not mean they are exempt from suicidal thoughts. Faith in Christ will not save your loved one from suicide. Faith will help carry them to a place or belief that it will get better, but faith alone will not protect them from the desire to commit suicide or the temptation to. Knowing that they are loved by God and by friends and family helps them deal with the depression and feelings of hopelessness.

Does Your Loved One Allow Space for Processing Their Emotions?

Are they practicing good self-care and attending therapy sessions? Are they able to express their feelings in a safe place? Do they have someone that they trust that you also trust to confide in? Maybe they don't want to have the conversation about suicide with you or maybe you're not comfortable having the conversation. As long as the conversation is happening in a professional/safe setting, that is all that matters. So, if they have a therapist, psychiatrist, or a mentor they trust, that will work. They need regular scheduled time to talk about their feelings and make sense of what's happening in their lives.

Do You Allow Space for Processing Your Emotions?

Don't forget that you will need help from time to time with your feelings and emotions as you are a caregiver and worried for your loved one and yourself. Use therapy sessions for vision planning and focusing on your relationships, finances, wellness, or anything else you are worried about. Support yourself with regular therapy sessions.

Are You Feeling Depressed or Suicidal?

Sometimes caregivers overextend themselves so much that they come to a point where they want to give up on life. Please, if this is you, reach out to someone today. Find someone else to take over the responsibilities of caring for your loved one and get the help you need today. There are so many wonderful care and support groups online. Please call the suicide prevention lifeline at (800) 273-8255. Someone who cares is waiting for you to call. Don't even hesitate if this is you. It's okay if you can't find the words to express what you need. By simply calling, you can start off by saying, "I don't know how to explain it but I feel overwhelmed." Being a strong person means asking for help when you need it.

Living in a Home or Assisted Living Is Not a Prison

The goal for your loved one is to live as independently as possible regardless if they are 18 or 81. They want to be in charge to some extent and they need to have some confidence in themselves that they are self-reliant. Self-reliance is one of the top skills we all need as humans to survive. The fact that mental illness, Schizophrenia, puts some restrictions on independence does not mean it should rob and take away all independence. It is quite the opposite.

My mother needed a lot of help in her teenage years. She was hospitalized for a couple of years at Winnebago and it took many months of trial and error to find the right medication for her (Clozaril was her saving grace!). After she was stabilized in the hospital, she entered into a program where she lived with an older woman, Betty, who was like a mentor to her. It helped Betty have someone younger around to help her move furniture or household chores that she could no longer do, and my mom was perfectly able to do so in her 20s. The relationship worked and she lived with Betty until she married my dad in 1969 and moved out. Betty and she lived together for almost five years. She kept in touch with Betty until her death.

I think had the program not been available, my mom would have done well in a CBRF (community-based residential facility) or group home. I think she needed someone around her to encourage her, ask her if she was taking her meds, and oversee things to make sure all was good in the world. Teens with Schizophrenia can live at home but only under the care and compliance of a psychiatrist and only if the parents set good boundaries from the beginning. What many parents do is forget about the boundaries and start with bribing their adult children, usually in the form of money. This only lasts for so long, and it is a poor form of boundaries, if any form at all. Please do not do this to your adult child. Please allow them the gift of living outside of the home and being independent if it's possible for them. Let them learn about life on their own. Do not shelter them and allow them to hide in their bedroom in your house. Sometimes some of the toughest love is walking away and saying, "Son, it's time for you to leave the nest."

The Problem With An Adult Child Living in the Home of a Parent

In this situation, the adult child is fully relying on the parent for all things including food, shelter, medication monitoring, and in some cases even proper bathing and cleanliness. Usually the "child" is unable to keep a clean bedroom, will put holes in the wall out of anger and frustration, and will downright ignore their parents because out of rebellion they deep down resent their parents for the cage they have been put in. This is not a healthy situation for the child or the parent. This is a situation where the boundaries are set aside, and in the name of "love," a parent is holding the child hostage by paying for all their bills and providing money for them to do activities that at times can lead to breaking the law, doing drugs, or drinking alcohol. This is not okay. This is actually causing more harm than good.

But What if My Adult Kid Ends up Homeless?

This is a real fear of any parent of a child with Schizophrenia. While it is possible, it is very rare. Most patients will eventually admit themselves to a hospital, seek medical care, and from there be placed in a home. The system is put in place for them to receive assistance, and they will be able to live under the care of a team that oversees their well-being. It is a holistic approach of care. While it isn't perfect, and many patients will go through a number of different doctors and social workers, it is the only way for your adult child to get the help they need.

You cannot act as a doctor, nurse, social worker, and parent. It is just not physically possible. I see many parents trying to do this on Schizophrenia.com forum and it absolutely breaks my heart for them because they have no life and neither does their child. Please don't do this. Instead call the county, call human services, and ask how to get help for your child. Many times, it requires you to lovingly step away and allow your child to be in control of their lives. It might require them to live in their car until they fall in a driveway and the ambulance takes them to the hospital, and that is Day 1 of them starting a new life of self-reliance.

Dealing With Ambiguous Grief When Communication Breaks Down

Ambiguous grief is grieving someone who is still alive. For many, it is the realization that the person you love is no longer the same as you have known him or her to be. It can be caused by their hallucinations or state of mind, or for whatever reason they are completely different from how you knew them before. They aren't able to love you like they loved you before. This can be a very difficult process to go through. An example of this can be found when a spouse develops dementia and no longer recognizes you. It is the deepest and most hurtful grief because that person is still alive but not able to have and offer the same love and interaction they once did. It's a shock to the system when you've loved someone an entire lifetime only to end with them being confused, scared, or angry. Maybe you can relate to this? You are not alone.

According to whatsyourgrief.com, there are five steps to cope with ambiguous grief, or the reality that you just can't have the same relationship with your loved one that you once shared. Williams states it as the following:

- **Remember that the present doesn't override the past.** This can be easier said than done, but it is important to remember that the person your loved one is now doesn't change the person they were. Even if their words or behaviors now are difficult or hurtful, even if your relationship has changed and is not what it was, this doesn't change the person they were and the relationship you had. Cherish those positive memories, write them down, create a scrapbook of old photos, whatever you can do.

- **Understand that the illness isn't the person.** This sounds obvious, but it can be really tough when someone you love seems like they should be the same wonderful person they always were and they're not. Whether it is addiction, dementia, a brain injury, mental illness, or anything else, it is important to understand the illness. As much as we may still feel anger, frustration, or blame toward the person, understanding the illness can divert some of those feelings.

- **Acknowledge the grief and pain of the loss.** Though society may not always recognize this type of grief, it is important that you give yourself permission to grieve this loss. Acknowledge and express the pain of the loss, rather than try to ignore or avoid the pain.

- **Be open to a new type of relationship.** When the person we love has changed, the relationship we have with them will inevitably change. This can feel like it is objectively and entirely a bad thing, but there is an opportunity for a new type of relationship. Will this new relationship always be easy? No. Hell no. In fact, many days it will be very, very hard. But being open and seeking gratitude in your new relationship can be extremely helpful.

- **Connect with others who can relate.** When many won't relate to ambiguous loss, finding a support group can be of help. There are support groups out there for caregivers of those with dementia, groups like Al-anon and Nar-anon for family members of those with addiction, and groups like NAMI (National Alliance on Mental Illness) who offer groups for family of those with mental illness.[3]

Check out more on Ambiguous Loss (www.ambiguousloss.com) by visiting the website of Pauline Boss, the woman who first labeled and researched this topic.

Questions:

1. What are your biggest communication problems with your loved one?

2. What three nonverbal communication options can you focus on to offer?

---

[3] Williams, L. (2014, October 16). *Ambiguous grief: Grieving someone who is still alive*. What's Your Grief?
https://whatsyourgrief.com/ambiguous-grief-grieving-someone-who-is-still-alive/

3. Are you grieving over losing the person that they used to be before the diagnosis? Do you feel grateful for the opportunity to love your family member or friend in a new way that embraces them for where they are at?

Coping with Caring for An Aged Loved One

My mother has had periods of sadness, especially after periods of highs. This is called Bipolar Disorder and 2.3 million Americans are affected by this condition. Schizophrenia and Bipolar go together sometimes. My mom has had times where all she does is cry on the couch. She does have extreme depression even now in her late 70s. She is not the same bright-eyed person she was even a year ago. Aging is just a really hard part of life. There are happy moments and sad moments. You have to learn to ride them out. Sometimes my mother changes from one day to the next. Sometimes she has a good week and is happy and dreaming about marrying Toby Keith. Other weeks she is filled with the terror of dying. As of late, that is how she's been. Every time I visit her she is aware of her drastic weight loss. Last week she was 88 pounds. No, that is not a typo. Over time, she went from being a healthy 150 down to the 90s. She stayed in the 90s for about two years, give or take. And right before Christmas she gave up all interest in food and we figured, well this has to really be the end. But it wasn't.

It's been six weeks since that happened, and although she's still here, she is more like a shell of herself. She said to me, "Becky, how did you get to be so big and how did I get to be so small?" She is right that she is super tiny and her body is failing her. Or she failed her body. Not sure which way it is. She is on a path to death, but she drastically wants off. She is like the scared toddler clutching at the side of a rollercoaster. She knows she must ride it out, but she wants no part of it.

How can I help my mom be okay with dying? Is it my job to? I have sat back in the chair, so to speak, for the last six weeks. I've watched her decline thinking, "Oh well. This is life." I almost took myself completely out of it. I had to check out for a while. I had to focus on my kids for a while and my own life. I had to be selfish. But right now, there's a real problem looming. The problem is my mother doesn't want to die but she's dying. And I have no idea how to change that. I've never helped a person die before! What the heck would I know? I'm 38 years old and worry about developing crow's feet. Not end of life stuff. But it seems every big decision in my mother's life was either made or influenced by my choices. It's a heavy burden to take on. Should I pull out all her rotting teeth at once or save a tooth one at a time? Should we fix her cataracts even though she's against it? Should we move her closer to us despite the fact she's thriving at her current nursing home three hours away and the move will more than likely cause a chain reaction of health decline and mental anguish? These are tough questions and ultimately decisions I had to make. Some of them I would later regret.

Yet God has equipped me to deal with this. Deep down I know the answer is in me. Because of my faith in Christ, my faith in the promise He made, I know the Holy Spirit lies within me. It is *in* me. The Holy Spirit is going to guide me today. I'm making it a plan to go to her nursing home and try to talk to her about death. We've talked about it before. The last time was three weeks ago when she explained, "I thought you were going to flush me down the toilet! I don't want to die! Don't leave me." That was very sad to hear. My mother who used to be so bold and fiery and full of zest was now the body of a small child telling me she's scared. It was the most hopeless feeling. I rubbed her back and told her there was nothing to be afraid of, that Jesus was making a room for her in His house and it would be the most beautiful place she's ever seen. Much better than this stinky nursing home!

Sometimes I feel like I don't know how to parent my parent. I know she needs love, reassurance, and patience. But she still needs her dignity. She is still my mother. No matter what faults she has, what illnesses she has, what weaknesses she has ... she's still my mother. "Lord God, help me to be a mother to my mother. Help me to show her the light. Show her Your love so that she doesn't have to fear death. Show her the beauty of believing in Christ's sacrifice for us." When you know this and believe this, death no longer has its sting! You are free. So, I guess right now all I can do is pray to God to give me the strength and the knowledge to *try* to help my mom. Help her relax and lean into Jesus. If I can do that, I've climbed a very big mountain.

The best way that I can share Jesus with my mom is through the gospel. So that is what I've been doing when I go to visit her. I pull out my Bible and read the scriptures to her. Her favorite is the book of Psalms. She asks me to read them again to her, over and over. Some days all she has patience for is a short devotional. That's okay! Do what you can for them. Just read the Bible to them. The more of the Bible that I've shared, the more healing my mom has had in her heart.

Easy Tips for Reading the Bible to a Loved One in a Nursing Home or Group Home

- Bring a devotional with you and read to them based on what is set out for that day.

- Use what you already take with you. Many iPhones and tablets have Bible apps that allow you to access the Bible without carrying the weight of it.

- Look up a passage ahead of time that deals with the emotion your loved one is feeling. Better yet, print it and put it on their wall or next to their bed.

- Leave a Bible for them in their room. If it's a sentimental Bible, like my mom's is, you might want to keep it in a special place outside of her nursing home so it doesn't get misplaced. Then find a Bible on sale that has no sentimental value and leave it in their room. Some nursing homes will even provide a Bible.

- Ask your church if someone could visit your loved one on a regular basis and just read the Bible to them.

Easy Tips for Sharing the Bible With a Loved One Who Lives Independently

- Call them up on the phone and share with them your daily devotional.

- Ask them if they need prayers. If they say yes, pull out your Bible and try to read a passage that may give them comfort. If you don't know where to start, start in Psalms.

- Write them a letter and share with them your favorite Bible verse. Maybe it will speak to them.

- Do not push a Bible onto someone who doesn't have a faith or want a relationship with the Lord. Instead, offer them your love and kindness. If they come to you and ask you, you can share the gospel with them.

- Ask them to come to church with you!

My mom kept a journal during her younger years while she was still living independently in her apartment. She often wrote about God, Jesus, angels, and the devil. She had questions like many questions I've asked. I wonder how wonderful it would have been for her to have a companion sit with her on the couch and talk to her about her faith. Unfortunately, that didn't happen for her. She struggled with understanding why God would allow pain in her life and in other's lives. If you wonder that too, you are not alone. My mom often said she felt sorry for the devils. I think that was her way of saying she feels sorry for anyone who falls away from the Father. I honestly feel the same way.

I don't think it's right for a son or daughter to run away from their loving Father, but if they do I think, "Oh that is so sad." I think of the Bible story of the Prodigal Son and how he ran away from his dad in his youth and didn't understand how young and foolish he was to take his dad for granted, to basically tell him he wished he were dead so he could get his inheritance early. And yet despite his foolishness, when he ran out of money, out of desperation and little hope, he came back to his father. He was expecting a door in his face, but instead his father ran to him in much anticipation and threw his arms around him and cried to his servant to kill the fattened cow and prepare for a great feast. That is how our Heavenly Father feels about those who fall away from Him. He wants us to come home to Him. He is waiting for us to say, "Lord, I messed up. But I'm here now. I want to make it better with You. I want You in my life. I need You." Oh how the Lord revels in that! He yells in heaven to prepare a feast for you and He rejoices gladly in you.

Who Is *Your* Support System?

Whenever we are in charge of taking care of someone else, we need to have a support system in place to take care of us. We've already talked about coming to the Father, and that relationship should be first in your life. After you hand over the big stuff to the Lord, is there someone or a group or a person who can help you achieve the small things? The small things matter. Let me try to explain.

Sometimes I need to make big decisions and I pray to the Lord to help me gather the information I need to make the right decision. Just this week, while social distancing for COVID-19, my mom's nursing home called me and asked for permission to test my mom for COVID even though she wasn't having any signs or symptoms. Normally I am very protective of my mom and I refuse all immunizations because of her weak system from all the medication she's on. Once I let her have the pneumonia shot and it landed her in the hospital for a week. Please don't read this and think I'm anti-vax. Everyone has to do what is best for them. I believe in vaccination, and I think we need to use all our current medical technology, but we have to use common sense. I could not tell the nursing home it was okay without further research. Instead I told the administrator I would think about it and get back to him by the end of the day and get the form back to him. I said a short prayer to God and asked Him for guidance. I first asked my spouse, and he said, "Yes. I would have her tested." My closest friend and Christian mentor also said yes and that it will be good for the nursing home to know. So, I agreed even though I hated the idea of them shoving a swab up her nose. I agreed the good and knowledge of it outweighed the bad of it.

Had I not consulted the Lord and my top two mentors, I would not have come to such a good decision so quickly. In life, sometimes we are called to make decisions and make them quickly.

Now, you might be saying, "But I don't have a spouse or a close friend I can count on." My quick answer is if this is true, then you need to work on creating good relationships in your life. Author and speaker Shasta Nelson wrote *Friendships Don't Just Happen*, and it's one of my favorite guides for creating good and healthy friendships. Her argument is that people don't just come knocking on your door and ask to be your friend (well not usually!) and so we have to put in a little bit of effort to make that magic happen. The older I get, the more I need good Godly women around me! I need help from a tribe. If you have children then you understand the concept of needing a village to raise a child. The same goes for you now that you are caregiving for someone else.

Now that you need to make sound decisions on someone's behalf, whether you are a legal guardian, parent, spouse, girlfriend, or friend, your role will take up great energy and will not go without worry. So, you need a support system you can trust that uses good sound judgement and biblical knowledge and power to help you make good decisions. If there aren't at least two people popping up in your mind right now then I recommend you get Shasta's book and start working on creating a base for yourself of sound friendships. We need connection in our lives. We need support. In return, the more you help these few important friends the more they will help you. I've spent many mornings on the phone listening to my friends and offering support during crisis moments or tough moments. It happens to everyone! Be the source of comfort for a good friend and they will give it back to you.

My mom knew how to be a good friend. She had lifetime friends, and they cherished her and she cherished them. These relationships didn't just last a couple months and then fizzle away. My mom was a loyal and loving friend. And people loved her for it. Elizabeth was her very best friend and they fought a lot. Sometimes they would both say things to hurt one another and not talk to each other for a few days, but eventually one of them would apologize and soon the other would and they would be back to shopping and drinking soda at Burger King. They used to say, "We're going bumming." This also used to irritate me as a child! "Why do you call it bumming?" I asked. "Because we are bumming around. We aren't doing much of anything except being with each other." What a beautiful concept. I realize now all I want to do is bum around with the people I love too. And love each other they most certainly did.

Evolving as a Caregiver

"You, O Lord, are a God full of compassion, and gracious, Longsuffering and abundant in mercy and truth."
–Psalm 86:15 NKJV

We are all evolving as a person and as a species every day. Either you are moving forward in your life or backward. You are either learning or forgetting. In life, nothing stays the same. Have you noticed this? If you want to be a faster runner, you need to put in the time and effort to run every day. If you want to be successful in business, you need to take a good chunk of your time and devote it to planning and business strategies. Whatever your goal is, it is only a dream until you put action to it. Then once you put in the work, you are working towards real goals.

This approach can be applied to caretaking as well. When you focus on your journey as a caretaker, when you take a step back and see where you've come from and where you are going, you can allow yourself to make good decisions about how to adapt and to change in your caretaking. These decisions moving forward will set the tone for your caretaking and will help you make the adjustments you need to thrive and continue care in a place where your cup is full.

Many caretakers don't take the time to do this. They are not evaluating because they are just going with the motions every single day. Like living paycheck to paycheck, they are reacting to life and to their loved one instead of staying on top and being proactive. Proactive caretaking will only happen if you've already started implementing the first steps outlined in this book of creating boundaries, accepting that you are not perfect, and then lastly having the discernment to know when you need to step in and when you need to stay back and to pray.

If you follow the foundations of my advice, and you are already operating at a balanced level, the last stage is being proactive in your care, and it can absolutely be achieved! Every person that needs care will fully benefit from a caretaker who is looking continuously for ways to improve their life. It's no different than if you were a principal of a school and you were in charge of a whole staff of teachers. In order to provide a well-run school, as a principal you need to be setting time aside for planning and vision and allowing space for new innovative teaching approaches. You need to be open to new technologies and looking at new incentives to pay your staff well. You need to look at the school from a holistic approach. You don't just wake up one morning and react to a problem.

This concept can be applied to caretaking. Are you simply giving away all your energy to caretaking? Are you forgetting to take time for yourself and practice good self-care? Are you still filled with guilt over making the wrong decisions over the reality of not being perfect? If the answers are yes, then you need to reread this book! You need to give yourself the grace and the self-love to acknowledge that you are not perfect and your caretaking is not perfect, but that through Christ, and help from the Holy Spirit, that you can and will make the right choices. That you will learn from your mistakes.

Real peace in the tough choices comes when you know you've taken the time to pray and get down on your knees and thank Him for the guidance and protection that He has already given to you. It was a free gift when you chose to put Him in your heart, when you chose to be His child. You have a right to tap into the Holy Spirit and to receive guidance even on your hardest day, especially on your hardest day. God wants you to tap into Him. God is waiting for you to lay down your weary arms and take rest in His perfect love. You can do this, and I will show you the three basic steps to start living as an evolved caregiver.

How to Evolve in Your Caregiving

A rookie caretaker may give away endless guidance and help without establishing good and healthy boundaries so that he or she is well adjusted and supported. An evolved caregiver is someone who understands the importance of boundaries and making sure they are well taken care of first before they even begin to look after someone else. Which would you rather be? It isn't easy to choose to be an evolved caregiver because it takes time and effort to make that decision! You need help, you need someone to show you what that looks like. Many of us don't naturally know that there's another way, a better way to be a helper. We only know what we know. If you have been operating more as a rookie caretaker, more by the seat of your pants, don't despair or beat yourself up! You couldn't help it. No one showed you how to do it. Today marks a new day. Today marks the beginning of your new mission in caregiving because today's the day you start taking care of yourself first.

When you start taking care of yourself first, when you have established healthy boundaries, when you've said no when you aren't comfortable, you are ready and well rested and able to take a step back.

1. Identify the problems before they become disasters.

I encourage you, after you've answered the questions at the end of each chapter and done the self-care exercises I've laid out, to get out your notebook and at the top of your page identify all the struggles of your loved one. Identify the problems in their life. For my mom, when she was still living at home, the problem was she wasn't able to take care of herself well because, for example, she couldn't cook herself healthy meals anymore. In this case, I would write that down as a problem. The solution could be several things. Maybe I could hire someone to come in and prepare meals. Maybe I could sign her up for Meals on Wheels delivery. Maybe it would be time to look into assisted living. By identifying the problems before they are disasters, I am being proactive in her care. I'm going to lay it all out; I'm going to take time to jot down all of my worries and concerns for her. Also, by doing this, I'm going to sleep better at night. I can't tell you how many nights I've lost sleep over worry. God doesn't want us to worry! He wants us to be healthy.

2. Pray over the problems and ask God for the solutions.

After you've identified the key problems, pray over them. Ask the Lord and Holy Spirit to show you all the possible solutions. Even if they are crazy at the time or don't make sense in the moment, don't delay. Write them out! Sometimes the answers have nothing to do with what you would think. For example, one time I prayed for solutions from the Lord to help me get more understanding from my husband. I wasn't feeling supported, and in fact, I was feeling abandoned. I prayed outside on my porch one day. I was sitting in nature with my notebook and Bible in hand, just letting the Lord know that I was frustrated in my marriage and I was willing to do anything to be on the same page with my husband. And I thought for sure the Holy Spirit would tell me to do something that was directly associated with my husband, but instead the Holy Spirit told me I needed to be more childlike and play more with my kids and take time to nurture my more juvenile self. (This is something I need to work on, being a naturally serious person.) Well that had nothing directly to do with my marriage, but once I started playing outside with my kids and swinging on a swing set, I felt support for myself and I was able to step away from focusing on what my husband was doing wrong and focus on what felt good, which was being a kid again. How profound and what a surprise! Only God knows exactly what you need in this moment. But you won't know what He's asking you to do if you don't take the time to sit at His feet and just ask for it. Ask for what you need. Ask what your loved one needs.

3. Thank God for His answers and believe that the problems have already been solved.

This is much easier said than done, but it is the most important step. It's believing that God has already moved mountains for you. He wants you to be living well, and He wants you to be balanced in your caregiving.

Mark 11:24 says, "Therefore I tell you, whatever you ask for in prayer, believe that you have received it, and it will be yours."

Once you have evolved as a caregiver, and you've decided to keep yourself in mind first, then you can create a reality where you and your loved one are both getting your needs met. God doesn't ask you to give yourself away, God asks you to give because you've already been given all you need through Him, and now you are offering your time that has been well sheltered to specific areas because you've been proactive in the above exercises and you know exactly where to put your focus.

Please do not compare yourself to other caregivers. No matter who you compare yourself to, you will always find stronger points in someone else and weaker points in someone else. That's because equality is not possible when comparison steps in. By faith and God's standards, we are all equal—equally His. We can spiritually say we are the same, we bleed blood the same, we all get hungry and require food, we all have humanistic qualities that resemble one another. But when faced with a spiritual battle where we are constantly comparing ourselves to others, we will most certainly always fall short. We will focus on our shortfalls, and we will believe the lie that we are less than.

This makes God so sad, the Creator of you and all your goodness and beautiful qualities. He sees you comparing yourself to others, and He sees that you are falling prey to Satan's temptation to believe you are not doing enough, working hard enough, or standing tall enough. Oh how much pressure we put on ourselves to prove to us and others we are perfect, smart, and capable people. Yet according to earthly standings, we will never measure up because of the sin in this world. The game is set up for inequality and unfairness from the very beginning. There is no way to hit restart on it. But we can boost our immunity in life by turning to God and the goodness of life and relying on His view of us to override other's views of us and the feeling of inadequacy. After all, when the wood maker is done building his project, is anyone else more deserving of criticizing his work other than himself? Then neither should we put focus on other earthly beings being authorities over our lives and how we view ourselves. In other words, we can find our self-worth through God. And only God, period.

Praise God that He makes it easy for us to know this knowledge! Praise God that we no longer need to be tired caretakers, that He allows us this time to focus on the planning and future of our loved one. I hope you start implementing this simple approach to problem solving for you and your caregiving.

Find Purpose in Your Caregiving

I recently had the opportunity to read the book *Just One Thing* by Gary Keller. In this book, Gary outlines the importance of being selective with your to-do list and furthermore discourages us from the temptation of multitasking and pouring ourselves too thin. Like having too many pots in the fire, your caregiving can suffer if you aren't intentional on what to focus on. This fact applies to virtually any area in your life. It can apply to your work or even your love life. People who are in the dating pool that have a hard time finding a date and sticking with that person are often requiring too long of a "must have" when finding a potential mate. Like the lonely woman who waits for prince charming to walk through the door, so can a caregiver never feel total accomplishment if they don't prioritize what is important to them.

Gary also says we should pick one important priority and put it into a to-do box. Everything else goes into a separate box. This allows us to be very efficient in achieving our top priority and to complete the tasks necessary to achieve that goal. When your mind is focused on one particular goal, everything else is pushed back, allowing you to quickly make progress. This is so important for when you create balance and confidence in your caretaking.

For example, in the beginning of being a guardian to my mother, I set goals to visit my mom once a week, help her clean her refrigerator once a week, help her move into assisted living, help her buy new clothes, help her to her doctor's appointments, help her buy hair dye, and the list goes on. Guess how confident I felt about my caretaking?! I felt like a failure ... I was never measuring up and the to-do list was getting longer and longer.

Now, you can say I was exhausted because I wasn't setting good boundaries. And while that is true and I discussed that earlier in the book, the important point here is not *what* I'm doing but what I'm *hoping* to do. What I am setting my eyes to do and to do well. I wasn't doing that. I was trying to multi-task and get it all done at once. I

WHAT YOU CAN DO TO MAKE A DIFFERENCE

thought it would be like a buy one get one free except it doesn't work that way at all. It just makes you feel like a failure and it makes you feel like giving up. Instead, since my mom's last move into her nursing home, I realized with everything on my plate including running my household with four kids, managing homeschool, and maintaining my marriage, I would need to get real about my priorities.

For me, the goal and main priority became to visit my mom once a week. I gave myself permission to visit her for a short visit, just enough to check on her and make sure she was okay. A long visit wasn't necessary unless she was able to connect with me. So I gave up the perfection of having to visit her multiple times a week (which is what I was doing previously) and instead focus on less visits that were shorter but more quality filled. I took pictures with her, read the Bible to her, prayed over her, told her I loved her. Sometimes I've been known to make it a goal to get her to laugh once. If I've done that I've done my job. Many times when I do go to visit her she's sleeping and that's okay too. I still met my goal.

Now I still want to do several other things for her like manage her payee, check in with her social worker, attend care conferences for her at the nursing home, buy her gifts on holidays, and set up a burial trust for her. These are all important tasks but not THE most important task. They will happen in due time. They are not the priority right now. In a week that could change. That is the beauty of prioritizing, it can be whatever you make of it. Whatever you set your mind to is a reality as long as you start with the one thing.

I do have two secondary goals with my mom. They are attending her conference meetings and praying for her daily. If I can make those two, I know I earned some extra credit. Helping keep these three goals in focus helps put purpose to my caregiving. It helps me feel good about what I'm doing for her and it also makes these goals achievable by narrowing down the few necessary tasks I need to do. Don't overwhelm yourself with endless to-do lists. Instead prioritize and make life easier for yourself. Once you do those three priorities well, you can always add more, but you probably won't. This won't mean you won't do more than three tasks at a time, it just means those are the things you keep in focus daily. It is very good to be disciplined, keep your top three goals in focus, and do those three goals well. That is the foundation to having a healthy self-esteem about your caregiving and what you are doing for your loved one.

The exercise I'd like you to do is get out your notebook and write out all of the tasks you are doing for your loved one. Then circle the top three most important. Star the most important task. Then for the next week, only focus on the top task. Slowly add in the other two, and before you know it, you will be the caregiver you set out to be. Don't forget to give yourself a pat on the back!

Questions:

1. Identify the top three problems facing your loved one. Can you be proactive now to avoid a disaster?

2. What is the one thing you can do to help your loved one today?

3. What are the top three things you must do this month ... this year ... etc.?

Healing Begins With You

"I pray that your love will overflow more and more, and that you will keep on growing in knowledge and understanding. For I want you to understand what really matters, so that you may live pure and blameless lives until the day of Christ's return."

–Philippians 1:9–10 NLT

In order to heal others, you need to heal yourself first. I'm not even going to pretend I've fully healed myself from the pain of my childhood nor from the responsibility of caring for my mother. But I will say that it is our responsibility to heal ourselves. It is our responsibility to take action and do something, even small steps one at a time to create wholeness and well-being.

There are many things you can do to create healing for yourself. Probably the number one most important thing to begin with is to get therapy for yourself. I think everyone can benefit from therapy, specifically talk therapy. I have seen the same female therapist for over ten years. We have developed a close relationship, and we trust one another. I know that her advice will help me, and I trust her to help me. This is sometimes difficult at first. If you have a therapist who you don't trust, ask yourself if there is a good solid reason why. If there is, please find a new therapist that you are open to receiving help from. If you know deep down it's your own insecurities that keep you from trusting anyone, including your current therapist, start with affirmations such as, "I know my therapist cares for me and wants the best for me. I'm willing and able to do what they ask of me. I am eager to heal." Many people are not willing to listen to a therapist. If this is you, recognize it, acknowledge your fear, and move through the fear. Healing and wellness will be well worth it.

My therapist has helped me to learn how to recognize major stressors in my life. Sometimes we cannot identify triggers or problems until we speak of it out loud. We all need to navigate through stress, talk about how to cope with stress, and talk about our lives so that they make sense to us. Having this outlet is super helpful for me and is a major resource that allows me to take a good hard look at my life.

The other helpful thing my therapist did was teach me how to take care of my wounded self, or also known as my wounded child. You may have heard of this concept before and laughed it off, but I don't believe it's a joke, I think it's a very important tool. There are several ways to heal your wounded child, either through therapy like I did or through books such as *Home Coming* by John Bradshaw or *Soul Healing* by Tammy Smith. I do not believe I've fully healed, and I think I'm still on the journey to healing. However, each month and each year I get closer. This is a journey and not a destination. I think as humans we are always evolving, learning, and striving for inner peace.

The next way I work towards healing is by feeding my body healthy foods. Nourishing whole, organic foods. I listen to my body and how certain foods make my body feel. For example, I don't eat bread because bread with gluten gives me headaches. I don't like feeling sluggish, and I don't like having to lose a full day or an afternoon due to nursing a migraine. I treat my body well by not eating foods that make me suffer. I encourage you to figure out what foods help heal you and make you feel good. A lot of people enjoy a diet of non-processed foods and whole foods, but this does require some meal planning.

An affordable meal planning program that I've personally used and that is backed up by financial expert Dave Ramsey is the online meal planning emeals.com. I like eMeals because you can pick a meal plan that works for you or your family, it connects to the app Instacart, and you can easily order groceries you need for the week in a matter of minutes. I don't know about you, but I've really stressed out over meal planning. This website will pick recipes for you and tell you what ingredients to buy if you enjoy grocery shopping, or if you don't, you can use the Instacart app connected to emeals.com and have your groceries delivered. Meal planning is a breeze, and this is a lot more affordable than ordering take out every night. And the benefits are you will feed your body the nourishment it needs. This is not an endorsement, just me being honest with you on how I keep my life sane with feeding and cooking for a large family of six. Plus, if you are caretaking for someone who is physically or mentally ill, think of how much this food will bless them.

If you or your loved one experienced a childhood where food was scarce, you may need to be especially aware of how meal planning is a crucial part of your well-being. For example, when I become hungry and food isn't readily available, I start to panic. I think I'm going to go hungry or I'm going to starve! This is known as getting a case of "the hangries." You become hungry and angry at the same time. This, I know, happens to me because deep down I have a fear there won't be enough food for me to eat. It is first a physical response to being hungry then ultimately it is an emotional response to being hungry. If you are someone who can relate to this and you feel you get an emotional response when you become hungry, I encourage you to leave snacks in your car or meal plan and make that a part of your healing journey.

Sleep is the next area of focus. You need to get enough sleep at night. Sleep is so important for good mental health. It helps you to function and think properly, and it gives you the energy to get a lot done during the day. If you are caretaking for someone else, you're going to need that extra energy. Everyone needs around eight hours of sleep at night. I know some people claim they need less, but I truly think all adults should strive for at least seven hours of sleep at night, and if you have a very heavy workload, I would add a couple of hours to that, or at the very least add in a 20-minute cat nap after lunch or 30 minutes of mediation to give your brain a proper amount of rest.

WHAT YOU CAN DO TO MAKE A DIFFERENCE

The last area of healing is to follow positive mentors on Instagram or social media. This can be anyone from a respected author or speaker or educator to maybe even a celebrity that focuses on positive mental health strategies. I personally enjoy watching the Holistic Psychologist on YouTube because she has a lot of great videos on how to do the work to heal yourself. She focuses on healthy ways to process your emotions and how to have successful and wholesome relationships with others. Being mindful and having that mindset that you're always willing to hear more and to learn more is so important because we are constantly learning no matter how old we get! We need to still have that child-like mentality of being open minded to learning new things. I would encourage you to check out positive pages on social media because social media can be a source of negativity if you aren't careful.

Another positive aspect of social media is to join caregiver groups online, and I will link a few that I have joined and participated in. I think it's extremely important to see others walking the same walk as you; it can be very healing when you don't feel as alone. This is especially important now during COVID when we are being discouraged to get together with others in a social setting. I think it's important that we branch out virtually and connect with others online and who knows maybe make a new friend! If you find yourself feeling negative from these groups after you join them, then please, I encourage you to either quit these groups or stop watching the content and only use them for a place to post your questions and receive the helpful feedback you're looking for. Limit your time and make sure you aren't on social media for large amounts of time but use it as a tool that can be helpful as you find challenges in your life or in your caretaking.

Do you find yourself easily triggered, maybe a thought or smell that takes you back to an unpleasant memory ... and when this happens it is difficult to recover? Sometimes it can take hours, or even worse, days, to move past negative thoughts about yourself. It might lead to you feeling guilty or lost. I know I have had this happen to me a number of times. The devil can be sure to attack me when I'm down, when I'm weak or sick or tired, he tells me what a failure I am. I know many people deal with this, too.

Dr. Carolyn Colleen came up with the concept of the F.I.E.R.C.E. 5, a helpful tool to help you snap out of the negative self-talk and instead ground yourself in the belief that you are transforming five minutes at a time. Many of us are so overwhelmed that we cannot afford to take it day by day. Five minutes is much more doable. I love this approach and highly recommend it. To learn more about this technique, you can follow her on www.carolyncolleen.com.

Facebook Caregiver Groups:

Caregiver Support Group:
www.facebook.com/groups/103001490399094/

Families of Schizophrenia Support Group:
www.facebook.com/groups/268866299859344

Mental Health Awareness and Support Group:
https://www.facebook.com/groups/1535872206658543

WHAT YOU CAN DO TO MAKE A DIFFERENCE

Anxiety and Depression Support Group:
https://www.facebook.com/groups/316710102096353

Dementia Caregivers Support Group:
https://www.facebook.com/groups/1516449868588963

Drug/Alcohol Addiction, Recovery, and Family Support Group:
https://www.facebook.com/DrugAlcoholAddictionRecoveryAndFamilySupport

Chapter 6
A FINAL PRAYER FOR YOU

---

*"Your promise revives me;
it comforts me in all my troubles."*
–Psalm 119:50 NLT

Now I'd like to take the opportunity to pray for you, my dear reader:

Dear Lord,

The reader of this book is putting their faith into You. They are looking for help through Your Holy Spirit to be the caregiver You created them to be. They are tired Lord. Will you please show them how to do that? Make it clear today. Don't keep them waiting any longer. Lord, you said in Deuteronomy 31:6 that we can be strong and courageous because You will never leave us nor forsake us. How beautiful You are Lord that You have given us this promise.

As the reader's friend, I am requesting on their behalf that You would heal all scars that formed physically and emotionally from Satan's lies that they are not good enough. I pray You would infuse Your love into them and help them to see themselves in the way You do. Your love is never ending, and because of Your love, we are able to bring love onto others.

Amen.

In Summary

Being a caregiver is one of the most important jobs God will ever give you. If you are struggling, just know that you must first believe change is possible or you will keep living in the same mess you're in. That is the first step, to truly see the crucial job God has called you to do.

Remember to seek the Father. Dive into your Bible. Consult the Holy Spirit. Pray for guidance and trust that God will provide for you and for your family. This includes praying for protection against evil and against those that are negative around you.

Always ask, am I safe? Are they safe? That will help you make the changes you need to make so you can create better boundaries in your life. Boundaries that are clearly set allow for you to achieve balance in your life and promote safety and true security. If you don't honestly know how to answer those two questions regarding safety, please consult someone you trust like a friend, family member, or therapist.

For the Schizophrenia Caregiver: Although there is no simple formula to follow when loving someone with Schizophrenia, I hope this book gave you the courage, the insight, and the motivation to give yourself breathing

A FINAL PRAYER FOR YOU

room to make mistakes and to always get up and try again. Never stop loving, calling, reaching out, or caring for your loved one. Show them through your endless love that you have their back. Even when they make you angry, even when they tell you they hate you, *especially* when they tell you they hate you! Show up and show them they matter. You will never regret trying your best, but you *will* regret not trying at all.

Lainey's positivity, faith, and courage helped her in her 55 year and counting fight with mental illness. She is still fighting today, and I will always remain hopeful for her and her health despite her mental and physical decline in her elder years. I know God is capable of all miracles big and small.

> *"You have given me many troubles and bad times, but you will give me life again. When I am almost dead, you will keep me alive. You will make me greater than ever, and you will comfort me again."*
>
> –Psalm 71:20-21

I hope this book encourages you to find the positivity in your situation, not the death sentence. As Christians, we are never promised to have perfect lives or go without any stress or heart ache. So many books on mental illness boast the scariest book cover photos, usually of broken brains, or worse, ugly green mental hospital hallways. None of those pictures showcase the truth of mental illness—that people who have mental illness are not disturbed or different—they are wonderfully knitted by God, they are creative and passionate, they are loving, and they are real.

My mom has one of the most debilitating mental illnesses possible, and yet she impacted my life in the most amazing way. She taught me what true love is, she taught me by example how to live like Jesus. I remember her telling me I could do no wrong in her eyes and that no matter if I did the most rotten thing in the world, she would still love me. Now I tell that to my kids. I hope my kids understand how much I love them. I know I could never do as good of a job as my mom did with me. Considering her illness, she was a rock star when it came to parenting. I can't imagine anyone doing a better job than her, and certainly she had every right to throw in the towel. My mother was not a perfect mother, but in a lot of ways, her humility and honesty are what made her so "perfect" in my eyes. She was perfectly imperfect. And I hope to one day be just as loving as her.

Thank You
FOR READING UNBINDING LOVE

*A Guide for the Caregiver
Who Has Nothing Left to Give*

Don't forget to get free access to my eCourse "Finding Peace in Your Caregiving" by visiting the link below. Now that you've read the book, it's time to put that knowledge into action!

**Get my FREE bonus at:
www.cheeringpastchallenges.com/10steps**

ACKNOWLEDGMENTS

There were so many amazing people who inspired me to write this book and who helped me to continually improve it. I especially want to thank my husband for always believing in me. Without you, this book would not have been birthed into the world. Thanks for your support and for making it great!

Special thanks to Miriam Cavanaugh for her precious illustrations in this book. Miriam, you truly have a God given gift. To see more of Miriam's art you can follow her community **Joyful Light** on Facebook and her personal blog **Joyful Light**.

Additionally, I'd like to thank the following individuals:

Chandler Bolt and the SPS (Self-Publishing School) Community for their help and support in making this book possible. Carolyn Bostrack for believing in me and encouraging me to write this book. Special thanks to my SPS coach Gary Williams, Editor Sky Nuttall, Jen Henderson with Wild Words Formatting, Mark Crandall with Heart Centered Marketing, Jenna Matz with JAM Design and Media for her beautiful cover design, graphics, and website design, Cody and Elaine Johnston with Reckless Media, Jen Groover, and Thrivent Financial.

Special angels that helped my mom and I on our journey:

Don and Joan Lee
Anne Romond
Bonnie Akan
Teresa Basiliere
Serenity Home and the Hollub Family
Jan Bednarek
Beth Anderson
Janita Larson
Jon Reiner
Uncle David
Aunt Ruth
Aunt Mary
Cindy Pleggenkuhle
Tammy Steier
Leanne Showers
Father Thompson
Christine Myer

And the many friends and family members who have supported us over the years! Thank you and GOD BLESS YOU!

Lastly, I want to acknowledge my children and the power of prayer. Each one of my children prayed, offered suggestions, and encouraged me to write this book for their grandma and for all the caregivers who read this book. You are covered in prayer.

ABOUT THE AUTHOR

Rebecca Stewart is a survivor of a traumatic childhood, a caretaker to her mother, and cheerleader to those that can't see the light at the end of their caregiving tunnel. It was in her caregiving that she experienced the lowest emotional pain of her life. In this place, she had an experience with the power of God that gave her the strength and guidance to find inner freedom in her caregiving and was called to share her 10 Steps to Finding Peace in Caregiving model inside her memoir *Unbinding Love* and course *10 Steps to Finding Peace in Caregiving*, but also build a community through her content creation on her podcast and YouTube channel *Cheering Past Challenges*.

Cheering Past Challenges is a community designed to empower caregivers that once felt powerless. The community seeks to step out of the burden, anxiety, and stress of caregiving and into the freedom and inner peace found through the *10 Steps to Finding Peace in Caregiving* pillars: faith, grace, surrender, and hope.

If you are seeking to find inner peace in your caregiving, know you are welcomed into the Cheering Past Challenges community with open arms. Head over to all podcast streaming platforms and YouTube to get more content.

CAN YOU HELP?

Thank you for reading *Unbinding Love*!

If you enjoyed this book,
please leave me an honest review
wherever you purchased the book.

www.ingramcontent.com/pod-product-compliance
Lightning Source LLC
Chambersburg PA
CBHW020906080526
44589CB00011B/467